Management Accounting:
an Historical Perspective

Management Accounting:
an Historical Perspective

R. H. PARKER

READER IN MANAGEMENT ACCOUNTING, MANCHESTER BUSINESS SCHOOL
FORMERLY P. D. LEAKE RESEARCH FELLOW IN ACCOUNTING
LONDON SCHOOL OF ECONOMICS

AUGUSTUS M. KELLEY · PUBLISHERS
NEW YORK 1969

© R. H. Parker 1969

First published in the UK in 1969 by
MACMILLAN AND CO LTD

Published in the United States by
Augustus M. Kelley · Publishers
New York, New York 10010

SBN 678 07001 6

Library of Congress Catalog Card Number
79–83155

Printed in Great Britain by
WESTERN PRINTING SERVICES LTD
Bristol

FOR

AGNELLE

Contents

	List of Figures	8
	Preface	9
1	General Introduction	11

PART ONE   ACCOUNTING FOR DECISION-MAKING

2	Cost Concepts for Decision-Making	15
3	Discounted Cash Flow	34
4	The Origins of the Break-Even Chart	59

PART TWO   HISTORICAL PERSPECTIVE

5	Select Bibliography of Works on the History of Accounting	75
6	An Accounting Chronology	127
	Index to Part One	165

List of Figures

3.1	Net Present Value Curves of Mutually Exclusive Investments	50
3.2	Net Present Value Curve of a Single Investment	52
3.3	Multiple Rates of Return	53
4.1	Costs, Receipts, and Profits (Henry Hess, 1903)	63
4.2	Capital, Profit, and Dividends (Henry Hess, 1903)	64
4.3	Sir John Mann's diagram (1904)	66
4.4	Shop Standards at Different Capacities (C. E. Knoeppel, 1920)	68
4.5	The Graphic Basis of a Budget (W. Rautenstrauch, 1922)	69

Preface

THIS book was made possible by my appointment in 1966 as P. D. Leake Research Fellow in Accounting at the London School of Economics and Political Science. It owes much to the stimulating environment of the School's department of accounting.

I am also much in the debt of all those librarians who have so ably supplied me with the often rather obscure books and articles I have had to consult whilst writing this book. I am especially grateful for the help I have received from the British Library of Economics and Political Science and from the libraries of the Institute of Chartered Accountants in England and Wales and the Manchester Business School.

Finally, I should like to thank Miss Valerie Clegg for typing numerous drafts of the manuscript.

R. H. P.

1 General Introduction

ACCOUNTING data can be used for stewardship reporting, for managerial control and as an aid to decision-making. Historically, the stewardship function has been by far the most important and not unnaturally this is the aspect with which most writers on accounting history have been concerned. There is some literature on the development of the control function of accounting but almost none on the decision-making aspect. The main purpose of this book is to attempt to fill this gap. The reason for the gap will become apparent from even a cursory reading of this book. It is simply that accountants cannot claim to be the originators of either the underlying concepts or the practical techniques. In general, economists have been responsible for the concepts and engineers for the techniques. The moral is obvious and one which has been clear to some accountants for a long time: accounting can only at its own peril cut itself off from ideas developed by kindred disciplines such as economics, engineering, and operational research.

Cost accountants have taken an unconscionably long time to understand and make use of economic and engineering ideas. What Morrell W. Gaines (see p. 23 below) called 'book-keeperish minds' have been all too influential in a profession whose historical roots lie in bankruptcy, executorship and auditing, all of which mainly involve the recording and investigation of past transactions. That the influence of historical accounting was far from dead even in the late 1940's is clear from the case study of an English accountant given by Bostock.[1] His accountant was trained in a professional office and was engaged mainly on audit work of a repetitive and routine character with the emphasis always on the 'watchdog' aspect of accountancy. The product of such a training

[1] C. Bostock, *Managing, Accounting and Profitability* (London, Pitman, 1960) ch. 1.

naturally tends to regard management accounting as of much less importance than audit, tax, executorship, bankruptcy, liquidation and secretarial work. The realisation that accounting could be used to help to run a business dawned slowly on Bostock's accountant and only some time after the last professional examination had been passed. Standard costing (by then nearly half a century old!) he discovered as a new field in which his eyes looked forward into the future rather than back into the past. It was not easy to find businesses in England which had systems of standard costing in use; none of his firm's clients had one.

The development of accounting for decision-making is discussed in this book under three headings: cost concepts; discounted cash flow; the break-even chart. The development of the last is discussed in detail only to the beginning of the 1930's, but the discussion of the first two topics includes some contemporary history. All are treated from the point of view of management accounting, but inevitably a great deal of attention is given to the contributions of economists and engineers.

Accounting for decision-making is only one part of management accounting: the relevant cost concepts for management control, for example, are *not necessarily* the same as those discussed in this book.[1] Management accounting itself is but a part of accounting in general. As a help to seeing management accounting in its historical perspective, the second part of this book contains a select bibliography of works on the history of accounting and an accounting chronology which attempts to show the main events of accounting history not only in their political environment but also in relation to the development of economics, law, management and taxation.

[1] Consider, for example, the difference between evaluating the profitability of a department and evaluating the performance of the head of the department.

PART ONE

ACCOUNTING FOR DECISION-MAKING

2 Cost Concepts for Decision-Making

THE beginning of wisdom in using accounting for decision-making is a clear understanding that the relevant costs and revenues are those which as between the alternatives being considered are expected to be different in the future. It has taken accountants a long time to grasp this essential point (and by no means all of them have grasped it yet). In this chapter we shall trace the development of such ideas, mainly by economists but also by a few accountants, engineers and practical businessmen, and shall discuss the reasons why so many accountants have found such ways of thought uncongenial.

ROBERT LODER'S FARM ACCOUNTS

Although there was no formal analysis until the nineteenth century, it is highly probable that the relevant concepts were unconsciously used by many businessmen well before this. We can only judge whether this was so where the records have survived. One example has been noted by Yamey: Robert Loder's farm accounts for 1610–20[1] show a combination of 'primitive accounting form with evidence of keen understanding of economic calculation for business decision-making'.[2]

Each year Loder attempted to calculate 'The whole Summe of cleare Proffits made upon my Farme' and 'Which of my landes yelded me greatest profit of those sowed with wheat, or of those

[1] *Robert Loder's Farm Accounts 1610–1620*, ed. G. E. Fussell (Camden 3rd series, vol. LIII, London, Royal Historical Society, 1936).
[2] B. S. Yamey, 'Some Topics in the History of Financial Accounting in England 1500–1900', in *Studies in Accounting Theory*, ed. W. T. Baxter and S. Davidson (London, Sweet & Maxwell, 2nd ed., 1962) pp. 19–20.

sowed with barly'. His charges against profits included the opportunity cost of the capital invested in the farm, or, in his more graphic phrase, the 'use of my stocke which lay as dead'. That he understood the distinction between avoidable and unavoidable costs is clear from the following passage:

... for carying of my wheat to Marquet, I may reckon it to stand me in but little more then my manes labour that goeth with my horses & in selling it, because my charge in keping my horses is never the more or lesse (so longe as I keep vj horses & a Teame) for they would be els idle in the stable: and the beannes or pese which they bring home at many times is more worth than my manes labour comes to, & sometimes lesse & sometimes nothing perhaps.[1]

Another example is also worth noting. In 1805–7 William Murdoch used coal gas to light the cotton mill of Phillips and Lee in Manchester. In an *ex ante* comparison of the cost of gas as against candles it was noted that 'the cost of attendance upon candles would be as much, if not more, than upon the gas apparatus; so that in forming the comparison, nothing need be stated upon that score on either side'. £550 was charged for 'the interest of capital sunk, and wear and tear of apparatus'.[2]

NEO-CLASSICAL ECONOMICS

The nineteenth-century political economists developed their concepts of cost in an attempt to understand the workings of the economic system, not as an aid to businessmen. Edwin Cannan of the London School of Economics expressed the general view when he argued that the practical usefulness of economic theory was not in private business but in politics.[3]

[1] Fussell, *Loder's Farm Accounts*, pp. 137–8. The year 1617 has been taken as an example.

[2] Thomas S. Peckston, *A Practical Treatise on Gas-Lighting* (London, Hebert, 3rd ed., 1841) pp. 99–100. See also S. Pollard, *The Genesis of Modern Management* (London, Edward Arnold, 1965) p. 220.

[3] E. Cannan, 'The Practical Usefulness of Economic Theory', presidential address to Section F of the British Association for the Advancement of Science, Belfast, Sept. 1902, reprinted in *Essays in Economic Method*, ed. R. L. Smyth (London, Duckworth, 1962) p. 188.

W. J. Ashley, Professor of Commerce at the new University of Birmingham, was not at all typical when he urged in 1908 that contemporary political economy should be enlarged to include a 'business economics' which frankly took for its point of view the interest of the individual businessman or business concern. The problem of cost accounts, he thought, was hardly one that could be left entirely to accountants, for it was fundamentally a question not of technique, but of policy – not how to get certain figures, but what figures to try to get, and how to combine them. It was a capital defect of general economic literature that economists had not yet taken the trouble to enter into the businessman's point of view.[1] And so cost accounting was developed mainly by financial accountants and engineers with little help from economists, much to the detriment of cost accounting and also, perhaps, of economic theory.

The first task is to disentangle the relevant ideas from the economic writings of the period before the First World War, remembering always that the context in which these ideas are to be found is that of theoretical political economy, not that of the more workaday world of the accountant and the engineer.

As early as 1838 the French mathematician Augustin Cournot pointed out that a monopolist will always stop production when the increase in expense exceeds the increase in receipts, i.e., in modern terminology, when his marginal cost exceeds his marginal revenue.[2] But for nearly forty years Cournot's writings were completely ignored by economists. It was not until the neo-classical reconstruction of economic theory which started about 1870 that similar ideas became generally accepted.

Jevons, who may be regarded as the first English neo-classical writer, pointed out the irrelevance of past costs in a famous passage:

A great undertaking like the Great Western Railway, or the Thames

[1] W. J. Ashley, 'The Enlargement of Economics', in *Economic Journal*, XVIII (June 1908) 181–204.
[2] A. Cournot, *Researches into the Mathematical Principles of the Theory of Wealth* (1838) trans. Nathaniel T. Bacon (New York, Macmillan, 1927) p. 59.

Tunnel, may embody a vast amount of labour, but its value depends entirely upon the number of persons who find it useful. If no use could be found for the Great Eastern steam ship, its value would be *nil*, except for the utility of some of its materials. On the other hand, a successful undertaking, which happens to possess great utility, may have a value for a time, at least, far exceeding what has been spent upon it, as in the case of the Atlantic cable. The fact is, that *labour once spent has no influence on the future value of any article*: it is gone and lost for ever. In commerce, bygones are for ever bygones; and we are always starting clear at each moment, judging the values of things with a view to future utility.[1]

The concept of opportunity cost was first formulated by the Austrian economist Friedrich von Wieser in his paper 'On the Relation of Cost to Value' (written in 1876 but not published until 1929).[2] In his book *Natural Value* (1889) he expressed the idea as follows:

To say that any kind of production involves cost simply implies that the economic means of production, which could doubtless have been usefully employed in other directions, are either used up in it, or are suspended during it.[3]

The first writers in English to publish the concept were the American economists Green and Davenport. 'As soon as we look more closely upon our varied resources and the individual activities of economic life', wrote Green in 1894, 'we discover that many of our good opportunities are limited in number and extent, so that before devoting the opportunity to a particular

---

[1] W. S. Jevons, *The Theory of Political Economy* (London, Macmillan, 1871) p. 159. Jevons's examples were topical and well-chosen. The *Great Eastern* (launched 1858) was a disastrous failure; the Atlantic cable was laid by the *Great Eastern* in 1866.

[2] 'Über das Verhältnis der Kosten zum Wert', printed in F. von Wieser, *Gesammelte Abhandlungen* (Tübingen, J. C. B. Mohr, 1929) pp. 377–404. See G. J. Stigler, *Production and Distribution Theories* (New York, Macmillan, 1946) pp. 159–160, and T. W. Hutchison, *A Review of Economic Doctrines 1870–1929* (Oxford, Clarendon Press, 1953) p. 156.

[3] F. von Wieser, *Natural Value*, trans. C. A. Malloch (London, Macmillan, 1893) p. 175; for the original see F. von Wieser, *Der Natürliche Wert* (Vienna, Alfred Hölder, 1889) p. 168.

activity it behooves us to consider from what other uses we are thus withholding it. Such consideration gives rise to the conception of opportunity cost.'[1] 'If', wrote Davenport in the same year, 'the choice lies between the production or purchase of two commodities, the value of one is measured by the sacrifice of going without the other.'[2]

By the end of the century 'marginalist' economics had triumphed. In England its most avid exponent was Rev. P. H. Wicksteed (1844–1927), theologian, medieval scholar and economist. According to the marginal theory, explained Wicksteed, what a man will give for anything rather than go without it is determined by a comparison of the *difference* which he conceives its possession will make to him, compared with the difference that anything that he gives for it, or could have had instead of it, will or would make. The skill of a business manager consists in expanding and contracting his expenditure on the several factors of production so as to bring their differential significances to himself into coincidence with their market prices.[3]

SOME EARLY WRITERS ON COST ACCOUNTING

The last three decades of the nineteenth century were marked not only by the development of neo-classical economics but also by what has been called a 'costing renaissance' in the English-speaking world. The reasons appear to have been declining profit-margins and the increasing scale and complexity of business generally.[4] It

---

[1] D. I. Green, 'Pain-Cost and Opportunity-Cost', in *Quarterly Journal of Economics*, VIII (1893–4) 228.

[2] H. J. Davenport, 'The Formula of Sacrifice', in *Journal of Political Economy*, II (1893–4) 567–8. See also his books, *Outlines of Economic Theory* (New York, Macmillan, 1896) and *Economics of Enterprise* (New York, Macmillan, 1925).

[3] The original version of Wicksteed's address is reprinted in Smyth, *Essays in Economic Method*, pp. 247–72; a revised version was printed in *Economic Journal*, XXIV (1914) 1–23 and reprinted in P. H. Wicksteed, *The Common Sense of Political Economy and Selected Papers and Reviews of Economic Theory*, ed. Lionel Robbins (London, Routledge, 1934) II 772–800, and American Accounting Association, *Readings in Price Theory* (London, Allen & Unwin, 1953) pp. 3–26.

[4] 'So far as the engineering trades are concerned it is probable that business in

has also been suggested that before this period factory managers in England were too excited over the potential of power-driven machinery to devote much effort to seeking out the answers to industrial accounting questions.[1] It was not until 1887, in fact, that there was published what its authors justly claimed to be the first attempt to place before English readers a systematised statement of the principles of cost accounting – *Factory Accounts* written by the electrical engineer Emile Garcke and the accountant John Manger Fells.[2] An anonymous reviewer of the book in the *Accountant*[3] claimed that it was 'more of a theoretical than a practical work' and 'more in the nature of a work on political economy than an ordinary every day business treatise'. Reading the book today these strictures do not seem to be at all well merited. If anything, one wishes that the authors had curbed a little their passion for specimen forms.

British accounting remained, however, 'dominated by the requirements of the merchant, all the formal training, all the prestige derived from him'.[4] Although Garcke and Fells were clearly aware of the importance of the distinction between fixed and variable costs and, as Solomons says, 'must be counted among the founders of the "marginal cost" school of thought',[5] economic ideas of opportunity cost and differential cost had remarkably

---

the first three-quarters of the century was so good that manufacturers paid little attention to costing methods. While the demand for machinery was great and the supply of engineers limited, there was no pressing need for economy but in the course of time brains and capital were attracted and competition became keener.' (R. S. Edwards, 'Some Notes on the Early Literature and Development of Cost Accounting in Great Britain – IV', in *Accountant*, XCVII (1937) 283. See also D. Solomons, 'The Historical Development of Costing', in his *Studies in Costing* (London, Sweet & Maxwell, 1952) pp. 17-20, and Pollard, *Modern Management*, pp. 245, 248.

[1] S. P. Garner, *Evolution of Cost Accounting to 1925* (Alabama, University of Alabama Press, 1954) p. 67.
[2] E. Garcke and J. M. Fells, *Factory Accounts* (London, Crosby, Lockwood, 1887). For biographical details see Solomons, *Studies in Costing*, p. 35.
[3] XIV (1888) 278.
[4] Pollard, *Modern Management*, p. 213.
[5] *Studies in Costing*, p. 36.

little influence on early cost-accounting thought and practice. Why was this so? One explanation is that cost accountants, then as now, did not read the writings of economic theorists. Even when they did, they, like Cannan, did not expect to find anything of direct application to their own work.[1] A second explanation is that a background of financial accounting with its emphasis on past averages was not conducive to a realisation of the importance of expected future increments. The scorekeeper did not regard making decisions as part of his function. As the Anglo-American accountant-engineer G. Charter Harrison pointed out in the early 1920's, the reason for the development of cost accounting along historical lines by professional accountants was that most of the work undertaken by them concerned past records and the investigation of past transactions.[2]

The cost accountant became in fact a victim of his own lack of imagination;[3] convinced that what was needed was the 'actual' cost of a manufactured product he became increasingly concerned with building up figures of total cost by means of overhead allocation. This philosophy was well expressed by Alexander Hamilton Church, an English electrical engineer who settled in the United States around the turn of the century (the italics are his):

> A production centre is, of course, either a machine or a bench at which a hand craftsman works. Each of these is in the position of a little shop carrying on one little special industry, paying rent for the floor space occupied, interest for the capital involved, depreciation for the wear and tear, and so on, *quite independently of what may be paid by other production centres* in the same shop. Then, in addition to this, there will be a separate debit representing those items of incidence which can only

[1] 'There is little to suggest that the course of accounting has been consciously influenced to any considerable extent by economic thought.' (G. O. May, 'The Influence of Accounting on the Development of an Economy', in *Journal of Accountancy*, LXI (1963) 11.)

[2] G. Charter Harrison, *Cost Accounting to Aid Production* (New York, Engineering Magazine Co., 1921) p. 229.

[3] T. Lang, 'Concepts of Cost, Past and Present', in Solomons, *Studies in Costing*, p. 74.

be treated as an average all-round charge ... whatever else is done, *every dollar of charges must be burdened into some item of work.*[1]

There were some cost accountants, however, who stressed the importance of the future. For example, in 1903 the American engineer H. L. Arnold published a book in which he set forth a number of examples of the latest American practice and his own views of the true object of cost accounting. Finding the costs of things which have been made was not, he claimed, the true object of cost forms and procedures. What has been has been and belongs to the dead past, which no man can change, but the factory accountant hopes by ascertaining the cost of past production to be able to predict accurately the cost of future similar production. He should have no desire to record the factory past, save as a guide to the best management of the factory in the future. The factory manager's real objective in cost-finding is the accurate prediction of future production costs and the object of all cost-keeping is to reduce production cost.[2]

It was from a climate of ideas such as this that standard costing developed as part of the 'scientific management' movement. The earliest detailed description of such a system (without, however, giving illustrative accounts) was given by John Whitmore in a lecture before the New York University School of Commerce, Accounts and Finance, in February 1908.[3] Important contributions were later made by the American engineer Harrington Emerson and the Anglo-American accountant-engineer G. Charter Harrison.

Emerson distinguished between two radically different methods of ascertaining costs: after the work is completed or before the work is undertaken. The first method, the old one, still used in most undertakings, not only delayed information until little value

[1] A. Hamilton Church, *The Proper Distribution of Establishment Charges* (New York, Engineering Magazine Co., 1916) pp. 51-2, 140-1.
[2] H. L. Arnold, *The Factory Manager and Accountant* (New York, Engineering Magazine Co., 1903) pp. 8-9, 18.
[3] J. Whitmore, 'Shoe Factory Cost Accounts', in *Journal of Accountancy*, XVI (1908) 12-25. There is a history of American standard costing in German: K. Weber, *Amerikanische Standardkostenrechnung* (Winterthur, Keller, 1960).

was left in it, but was also 'wholly and absolutely incorrect' in that it mixed up costs and avoidable losses. The second method, on the other hand, facilitated 'an almost inexorable elimination of inefficient conditions of all kinds, standard expenses being constantly standardized at new levels – wastes, the excess above standard cost, being constantly removed'.[1]

There were even a few early writers on cost accounting who showed a good understanding of the use of differential costs. Three such who deserve to be remembered were the American engineers A. M. Wellington and Morrell W. Gaines, and the Scots chartered accountant Harold G. Judd.

Wellington was an American civil engineer who in 1877 wrote a standard work on *The Economic Theory of the Location of Railways* (New York, The Railway Gazette, 1877). A much revised and enlarged second edition was published ten years later in 1887. In it, Wellington pointed out that the most important problem of railway construction was whether or not to build a line at all. This was not an engineering question but one of finance and business judgement, to be settled by a more or less exact or visionary estimate of the available capital for construction, the probable gross and net receipts, and the resulting direct and indirect advantages to the projectors, with the final conclusion that (i) there is (or is not) sufficient need of a railway to give a fair return on the expenditure of a certain gross amount in constructing it and (ii) this gross amount can (or cannot) be raised. Once the decision has been made, the engineer should consider only the effect of his actions upon the *differences* in gross receipts, operating expenses and annual charges.[2]

Gaines's article carried the rather uninspiring title, 'Tabulating-Machine Cost-Accounting for Factories of Diversified Product', which probably has something to do with the undeserved oblivion

---

[1] H. Emerson, *Efficiency as a Basis for Operation and Wages* (New York, Engineering Magazine Co., 1909) pp. 149–50. On Whitmore, Emerson and Harrison see Solomons, *Studies in Costing*, pp. 42–5, 50.

[2] A. M. Wellington, *The Economic Theory of the Location of Railways* (New York, Wiley, 1887) pp. 13, 17.

into which it has fallen. He begins by pointing out that cost-accounting analysis has on the whole been slighted in favour of cost-accounting method although the latter must in theory be based upon, and derive its validity from, the former. A cost system has both a negative aim – the curtailment of waste and expense – and a positive aim – the making of increased profits through knowledge of profit-bringing qualities and conditions. It is the latter which is vital but the former although merely incidental is often the more emphasised. But, insists Gaines, 'Factories are run to make money and not to practise economies'.

After pointing out that the use of 'tabulating-machines' permits the same set of facts to be classified in several different ways, he goes on to develop his ideas of cost accounting as the provider of a profit criterion:

All knowledge of potential profits that experience may teach or reason create is, reduced to its lowest terms, no more than knowledge of the net difference in profit or loss which may be expected to follow choice between given lines of action. To determine this net difference with the greatest practicable accuracy is the main object of a cost system. For the profit-criterion, the fundamental principle is accordingly that of measuring differentials. This is a very different matter from the measurement of absolute quantities, to which cost systems too much confine themselves.

... Further, since it is obvious that only that part of the receipts or expenses which is influenced by a given choice of action needs to be subjected to measurement in order to determine the resultant net profit or loss, a sharp, and most important, distinction is to be drawn between those receipts and expenses that are 'direct' with respect to the course of action in question and those that are 'indirect'. All that will not vary with the choice of action are to be altogether discarded from consideration.

The usual total-cost figures prepared by cost accountants contain in 'indiscriminate burial' factors that vary with change of quantity and factors that do not, and such figures are therefore not adapted for measuring profit differentials. Conclusions based on them are always somewhat wrong and are sometimes totally misleading. The question of the proper apportionment of indirect charges can be avoided by using the differential plan.

Gaines points out clearly that in choosing between lines or in changing prices of lines a net profit approach is misleading; what is important is the contributions brought in by sales of individual articles towards the general upkeep of the establishment. It is the weakness of the net-profit-per-line approach that the tax for the general upkeep is subtracted before comparison is made, so that what is finally compared is the resultant of two factors that obey separate laws of variation.

As might be expected, Gaines is not in favour of full cost pricing. He thinks prices are ordinarily determined more by the market than by what a manufacturer *wants* to get. Where possible, prices should be set to bring in the maximum total of net revenue:

Absolutely the only use of the complicated addition of arbitrary percentage loading to cover indirect charges is that the process, being similar to that of competitors, gives an approximate idea of the price they will make in competition.

– but the arbitrary loadings may not be the same in different factories.[1]

In an address before the Glasgow Chartered Accountants Students' Society[2] Judd declared that cost accounts were valuable not only because they told what a job had cost in the past but as data for ascertaining what might be done in the future. Oncost was generally divided into 'direct expenses' and 'indirect expenses', but Judd doubted if this was sound. His preferred distinction was between 'fixed' and 'fluctuating' oncost. There was little point in distinguishing between works or factory expenses and selling, distribution and management expenses. The important distinction was not where oncost was incurred but how far it was absolutely

---

[1] Morrell W. Gaines, 'Tabulating-Machine Cost-Accounting for Factories of Diversified Product', in *Engineering Magazine*, xxx iii (Dec. 1905) 364–73.
[2] Harold C. Judd, 'Fixed and Fluctuating Oncost', in *Accountants' Magazine*, Mar. 1914, pp. 134–46.

fixed and how far it was the kind of expense which fluctuated up and down.

Judd gives as example the manager of a business who goes down to the Exchange one day and is offered a contract of 500 tons of iron at 100s per ton. Before going to the Exchange he had been told by his accountant that the cost was running at 105s a ton. What the manager should do is to go back to his accountant and ask how the cost of 105s had been arrived at. The accountant may explain that direct materials and labour cost 80s and oncost 25s. If the latter figure is dissected it may show that 10s is fluctuating oncost and 15s fixed oncost. Now, asks Judd:

> If that man gets a price of 100s per ton, what is the result? He has covered his Direct Cost and his Fluctuating Oncost, and he has got 10s over to account of his 15s of Fixed Oncost. If the manager knew that much at the time he would have known that in taking the contract at 100s he was getting a contribution of 10s a ton towards reduction of Oncost that is inevitably running on whether he gets work or not. The 'contribution to Oncost' is thus in reality 10s per ton, and not 20s per ton as first appeared; that is, he can without loss book orders down to 90s per ton, but anything below that is at an actual loss. With such information before him the manager knows how near he can sail to the wind without making undue leeway.

J. M. CLARK'S 'STUDIES IN THE ECONOMICS OF OVERHEAD COSTS'

It was not until 1923 that an economist took a close look at cost accounting. J. Maurice Clark's *Studies in the Economics of Overhead Costs* was a work of great importance to the cost-accounting profession but, for the reasons already discussed, it had little immediate practical impact. In this section we shall outline Clark's views on cost accounting. In the next section we shall survey the writings of those few accountants who, much in advance of their time, did understand and seek to propagate the relevant concepts of cost.

Cost accounting was, wrote Clark, still in its formative stage[1] but it already had a voluminous literature and at least one of the characteristics of a science – that of being inscrutable to the uninitiated. There were, he saw, great opportunities for the development of arbitrary and fictitious notions of cost, through the necessity of apportioning items somehow even if there was no scientific basis on which to do it.[2]

The terminology of costs was in a state of much confusion but it was not possible to solve this confusion by discovering and adopting the one correct usage. There was no one correct usage since usage is governed by the varying needs of varying business situations and problems:[3]

As a result, if cost accounting sets out, determined to discover what the cost of everything is and convinced in advance that there is one figure which can be found and which will furnish exactly the information which is desired for every possible purpose, it will necessarily fail, because there is no such figure. If it finds a figure which is right for some purposes it must necessarily be wrong for others.[4]

In a phrase: 'different costs for different purposes', the title of chapter 9 of Clark's book.

An interesting example of the failure to realise the need for different costs was the contemporary discussion among cost accountants on interest on capital,[5] a discussion which Clark found 'a strange mixture of dogmatic assertion and arguments from expediency'.[6] In his own discussion of some typical problems (whether or not to build a plant; how large to build it; whether to change the methods of production; income available for dividends; differential cost of added output; temporary shutdown; whether to add a side line; abandonment) Clark showed that

---

[1] The Institute of Cost and Works Accountants (U.K.) and the National Association of (Cost) Accountants (U.S.A.) had both been established in 1919.
[2] J. Maurice Clark, *Studies in the Economics of Overhead Costs* (Chicago, University of Chicago Press, 1923) p. 14.
[3] Ibid. p. 175.
[4] Ibid. p. 234.
[5] Summarised in Garner, *Evolution of Cost Accounting to 1925*, pp. 142–61.
[6] Clark, *Overhead Costs*, p. 255.

interest on capital was sometimes a relevant cost and sometimes not. For example, if a business is deciding whether or not to build a plant, interest on the entire investment needs to be taken into account; the cost of continuing in business, rather than going out permanently, includes interest on the salvage value of the investment only; the differential cost of added production may include much or little interest according to the conditions of the case. Interest should therefore be included in the raw data gathered so that managers can make comparisons of alternative costs.[1]

COST ACCOUNTING BETWEEN THE WARS

Set against Clark, cost-accounting theory and practice in the 1920's and 1930's is very disappointing. John J. W. Neuner's *Cost Accounting. Principles and Practice*[2] can fairly be taken as representing the best practice of the period. Neuner did recognise, in the course of a discussion on interest as a cost, that

> items to be included in or excluded from cost depend entirely upon the purpose for which the cost figure is to be used. There is no such thing as *a* correct cost figure for *all* purposes.[3]

Later, however, after stating that a producer of joint products will attempt to establish selling-prices for each so that the maximum profit will be realised on the total production, he suggests quite wrongly that this can be achieved by allocating the cost of manufacturing to various joint products on 'some reasonable basis'.[4]

The really notable feature of Neuner's text is the inclusion as the last chapter of the early editions of a 're-examination of cost accounting from the managerial viewpoint'. This was written by

[1] Ibid. ch. 9.
[2] J. J. W. Neuner, *Cost Accounting. Principles and Practice* (Chicago, Business Publications Inc, 1939). This book is now in its 7th edition (1967); editions since the 2nd (1942) have been published by Richard D. Irwin.
[3] *Cost Accounting* (2nd ed., 1942) p. 277.
[4] *Cost Accounting* (2nd ed., 1942) pp. 450-1. Similar statements are made in the 6th ed. (1962) ch. 16.

W. J. Vatter and is a great advance on anything which had been published in a cost-accounting text before this date. Vatter[1] points out that practically nowhere in the literature of cost accounting is there more than an elementary attempt to explain the meaning of the word 'cost'. He then goes on to stress the importance of understanding the concept rather than defining the word. The central idea is that of giving up, parting with, or sacrificing some thing or value to acquire some thing or value, but

There is no one cost which will fit all purposes any more than there is a single wheel which will fit watches, motor trucks, and railway trains.

After a series of examples illustrating the practical importance of information concerning total-cost behaviour, differential costs, imputed costs, replacement costs, sunk and out-of-pocket costs, and opportunity cost, he concludes that the *useful* cost accountant

must be able and willing to secure the kind of data which management may require for the many and varied purposes cost data may serve. He must determine how total costs behave at various levels of production for the product. He must be able to determine differential costs where the situation demands their use. He must know when to use imputed costs and replacement costs; he must understand the difference between sunk and out-of-pocket costs; and he must recognise the need for the use of such concepts in attacking special problems. The mere grinding out of figures according to a stereotyped plan is not cost accounting and should not be referred to as such.[2]

The cost accountant is thus called upon not only to find costs, but to know what costs to use.[3]

Similar ideas were beginning to be put forward by academic accountants on the other side of the Atlantic.

In 1937 R. S. Edwards delivered a lecture at the London School of Economics and Political Science on the rationale of cost

---

[1] *Cost Accounting* (1st and 2nd eds) ch. 29.
[2] Neuner, *Cost Accounting* (1st ed.) p. 696.
[3] Cf. Ashley's comments in *Economic Journal* (1908), quoted at the beginning of this chapter.

accounting.[1] The most important thing about costs, he argued, was the extent to which they changed with output. Most textbooks were still prone to emphasise that cost accounting analyses *past* costs, not future estimates, and did not make clear that data about the past were useful only in so far as they were a guide to future costs. It is, wrote Edwards,

future variable cost which is important . . . cost accountants can ignore expenses which are completely unchangeable . . . depreciation [and] every other expense must be examined in order to establish the relationship between changes in cost and output variations.

Profitability should be tested by comparing increments to cost with increments to revenue, rather than by totals and averages. Accountants have spent too much effort in trying to arrive at total cost 'by building up complicated and delicate oncost structures which depend on arbitrary assumptions'. Like Gaines, Edwards believed that in tendering for orders knowledge of market conditions was more important than estimates of total cost; methods of computing oncost vary so much that it would be dangerous to suppose that one's competitors have allowed roughly for the same oncost as oneself.

Ideas similar to those of Edwards were developed at greater length by his colleague R. H. Coase in a series of articles in the *Accountant* of 1938.[2] Coase stressed that attention ought to be concentrated on the variations in costs or receipts which will result if a particular decision is taken and that costs and receipts which will remain unchanged whatever decision is taken should be ignored.

He gave as an example a department store whose managers were discussing whether or not to close a particular department. A decision could not be reached because there was no agreement on the allocation to be made for rent to the department. Coase

[1] R. S. Edwards, 'The Rationale of Cost Accounting', in *Some Modern Business Problems*, ed. Sir Arnold Plant (London, Longmans, Green, 1937), reprinted in Solomons, *Studies in Costing*.
[2] R. H. Coase, 'Business Organisation and the Accountant', in *Accountant*, XCIX (1938); reprinted in Solomons, *Studies in Costing*.

pointed out that since in this case the amount of rent to be paid would remain the same whether the department was closed or not the question of rent allocation was irrelevant. All that was necessary was to discover what changes in costs and receipts would occur if the department were closed down, including those of any other departments affected.

This conclusion was attacked by Bigg, who was clearly thinking in terms of net profit per department and thought that Coase's methods were 'inequitable' to the other departments.[1] Bigg's views are interesting because they show how a background of financial accounting and auditing can lead to ways of thought wholly unsuitable for management accounting. For purposes of external reporting a reasonable case can be made for the use of total unit costs and obviously in auditing the ideas of fairness and equity are fundamental, but such ideas are just not relevant when the problem is to maximise the profits of the business as a whole. The *relevant* theory for this problem was in fact clearly stated by W. T. Baxter in an article in the same volume of the *Accountant*.[2] Baxter pointed out that the reasons for preparing departmental statements are (i) to find out whether each department is sufficiently profitable to justify its continuance, (ii) to find out whether the heads of the individual departments are avoiding unnecessary expense, and (iii) (in some cases) to find suitable selling-prices for the individual articles in which the department deals. There was no point in allocating any overhead expenses which would remain undiminished even if a department were abandoned and over which departmental heads had no control. A manager should ask, not whether the sale price of an article exceeded its average 'cost' (which might vary enormously by altering the method of allocation) but whether the business was making more profit by selling that article at that price than it could by adopting any other policy.

[1] See his letters to the *Accountant*, XCIX (1938) 539 and 795. For Coase's reply see pp. 705-7 (pp. 137-41 of the Solomons reprint).
[2] W. T. Baxter, 'A Note on the Allocation of Oncosts between Departments', in *Accountant*, XCIX (1938) 633-6; reprinted in Solomons, *Studies in Costing*, pp. 267-76.

COSTING LITERATURE AND PRACTICE SINCE 1945

Since the end of the Second World War the literature and practice of cost accounting, particularly in the United States, and to a lesser extent in Britain, has shown a growing awareness of the relevant costs for decision-making. The American evidence has been well set out by James S. Earley[1] and need not be repeated in detail here. Important contributions include the research studies published by the National Association of (Cost) Accountants[2] and the writings of Vatter[3] and Devine.[4]

Progress in Britain was slower, Solomons's study on 'Cost Accounting and the Use of Space and Equipment'[5] being one of the few examples of the application of opportunity costs. The official and less imaginative approach can be found in the Institute of Cost and Works Accountants' *Terminology of Cost Accountancy* (1952) where 'cost' was tamely defined as 'the amount of expenditure incurred on a given thing'.[6]

By the beginning of the 1960's the time was ripe for a new type of cost-accounting textbook, one which would emphasise decision-making and the different-costs-for-different-purposes approach. The need has been met in the United States by such books

[1] James S. Earley, 'Recent Developments in Cost Accounting and the "Marginal Analysis"', in *Journal of Political Economy*, XLIII (1955) 227–42, and 'Marginal Policies of "Excellently Managed" Companies', in *American Economic Review*, XLVI (1956) 44–70.

[2] For example those on 'The Uses and Classification of Costs' (Research Series no. 7, 1946) and the 'Assignment of Non-Manufacturing Costs for Managerial Decisions' (Research Series no. 19, 1951) reprinted in Solomons, *Studies in Costing*.

[3] W. J. Vatter, 'Accounting Measurements of Incremental Cost', in *Journal of Business*, XVIII (1945), reprinted in Solomons, *Studies in Costing*; 'Tailor-Making Cost Data for Specific Uses', in *N.A.(C.)A. Bulletin*, 1954 Conference Proceedings, reprinted in *Readings in Cost Accounting, Budgeting and Control*, ed. W. E. Thomas (Cincinnati, South-Western Publishing Co., 2nd ed., 1960).

[4] C. T. Devine, *Cost Accounting and Analysis* (New York, Macmillan, 1950). The relevant parts of Joel Dean's *Managerial Economics* (Englewood Cliffs, N.J., Prentice-Hall, 1951) were also very influential.

[5] *Accountant*, 27 Mar. and 3 Apr. 1948, reprinted in Solomons, *Studies in Costing*.

[6] In the latest (Oct. 1967) edition of the *Terminology* this has been slightly improved to read: 'The amount of expenditure (actual or notional) incurred on, or attributable to, a given thing.'

as C. T. Horngren's *Cost Accounting. A Managerial Emphasis*,[1] G. Shillinglaw's *Cost Accounting: Analysis and Control*[2] and C. L. Moore and R. K. Jaedicke's *Managerial Accounting*.[3] No comparable books have yet appeared in the United Kingdom.

SUMMARY

The concepts of cost relevant to decision-making were first formulated by the neo-classical economists at the end of the nineteenth century. The impact of their ideas on accounting thought and practice was delayed partly by the fact that the economists were not writing for, and consequently were not read by, practising accountants, engineers and businessmen; and partly by the historical bias which most accountants derived from the nature of their daily work.

It was not until 1923 that the economist J. M. Clark in his book *Studies in the Economics of Overhead Costs* took a close look at cost accounting. Unfortunately his views had little influence for a long time and it is only in the 1960's that it can be claimed with any justification that incremental and related concepts of cost have become an accepted part of the theory and practice of management accounting.

[1] Published by Prentice-Hall; 1st ed., 1962, 2nd ed., 1967. In 1966–7 this was the most commonly used text in cost-accounting courses at American collegiate schools of business (see Merrill B. Dilley, 'Textbooks Used in Accounting Courses', in *Accounting Review*, XLII (Oct. 1967) 801).
[2] Published by Richard D. Irwin; 1st ed., 1961, revised ed., 1967.
[3] Published by South-Western Publishing Co.; 1st ed., 1963, 2nd ed., 1967.

3 Discounted Cash Flow

In order to evaluate an investment decision it is necessary not only to forecast the relevant cash inflows (revenues) and outflows (costs) but also to allow for the time value of money. In other words, a discounted cash flow approach is required. In the previous chapter we discussed the relevant concepts of cost; in this chapter we survey the development of discounted cash flow criteria of investment evaluation. No attempt is made to discuss the problem of the cost of capital or the difficulties caused by risk and uncertainty.

The technique of discounted cash flow requires both an understanding of compound interest and an ability to set out the cash inflows and outflows likely to result from a particular decision to invest. Knowledge of compound interest goes back at least as far as the Old Babylonian Period (*c.* 1800–1600 B.C.) in Mesopotamia.[1] Setting out the cash implications of an investment is more difficult. It is not surprising that the earliest applications of discounted cash flow were to loans, where the cash outlays and receipts were known, and to life insurance, where probabilities could be calculated from historical evidence. The extension of discounted cash flow to investment in fixed assets came much later and was based on the work of engineers and economists. We therefore have to consider developments in three fields: actuarial science, engineering economy and political economy. They will be discussed in the order stated.

TRENCHANT, STEVIN AND THE BIRTH OF ACTUARIAL SCIENCE

In spite of the medieval Christian Church's ban on usury, European books on mathematics from Leonardo of Pisa's *Liber Abaci*

---

[1] O. E. H. Neugebauer, *The Exact Sciences in Antiquity* (Copenhagen, Ejnar Munksgaard, 1951) p. 33.

(1202) onwards contained problems concerning compound interest.[1] Before the sixteenth century A.D., however, interest *tables* were treated as highly confidential and existed only in manuscript. One of these early manuscript tables, composed about 1340, has been preserved in a copy made in 1472. It was prepared for the Florentine firm of the Bardi by Francesco Balducci Pegolotti as part of his *Pratica della Mercatura* which was not, however, published until 1766.[2] It is an interesting coincidence that the oldest accounting records definitely kept in double entry – those of the *massari* or stewards of the commune of Genoa – also date from 1340. Pacioli's *Summa de Arithmetica Geometria Proportioni et Proportionalità* (1494) contains a number of problems on simple and compound interest, mentions tables and sketches the way they should be computed, but it does not contain any tables.[3]

It was at Antwerp and Lyons, the two greatest financial centres of Western Europe in the sixteenth century, that interest tables were first printed. The first writer to provide them was Jean (or Jan) Trenchant in his *L'Aritmétique departie en troys livres*, published at Lyons in 1558. Two chapters (book 3, chapters 8 and 9, pages 235–55) discussed geometric progressions and compound interest. Tables were provided for $10^7 (1 \cdot 04)^n$, $n = 1, 2, \ldots, 40$ and $10^7 s_n | 0 \cdot 4$, $n = 1, 2, \ldots, 41$.

The second writer to include interest tables in a book was the famous Dutch mathematician, scientist, engineer and accountant Simon Stevin (1548–1620). Stevin was the first author to give a systematic treatment of decimal fractions and he wrote an influential book on double entry as well as important books on engineering.[4] *Tables of Interest*, published at Antwerp in 1582, was

[1] *Liber Abaci. Scritti di Leonardo Pisano*, ed. B. Boncompagni, II (1862) 267.
[2] *Franceso Balducci Pegolotti. La pratica della mercatura*, ed. A. Evans (Cambridge, Mass., The Medieval Academy of America, 1936) pp. ix, xiv, xi, xv, 301–2.
[3] Luca Pacioli, *Summa de Arithmetica Geometria Proportioni et Proportionalità* (Venice, 1494; 2nd ed., Toscolano, 1523) 1st part, 9th distinctio, 5th tractatus. See *The Principal Works of Simon Stevin*, ed. D. J. Struik, vol. IIA, Mathematics (Amsterdam, C. V. Swets & Zeitlinger, 1958) p. 14.
[4] On Stevin see O. ten Have, 'Simon Stevin of Bruges', in A. C. Littleton and B. S. Yamey, *Studies in the History of Accounting* (London, Sweet & Maxwell, 1956), and G. Sarton, 'Simon Stevin of Bruges (1548–1620)', in *Isis*, XXI (1934)

his first book. It is, in effect, a text on financial mathematics. Simple and compound interest are defined and explained and illustrative problems are worked out. The tables used for the solution of the compound-interest problems include:

$10^7(1+i)^{-n}$, $i = 0·01, 0·02, \ldots, 0·16$; $i = \frac{1}{15}, \frac{1}{16}, \ldots, \frac{1}{22}$; $n = 1, 2, \ldots, 30$; $10^7 a_{n|i}$, $i = 0·01, 0·02, \ldots, 0·16$; $i = \frac{1}{15}, \frac{1}{16}, \ldots, \frac{1}{22}$; $n = 1, 2, \ldots, 30$; $10^7(1+\frac{1}{15})^n$, $n = 0, 1, \ldots, 30$; and $10^7 s_n|\frac{1}{15}$, $n = 1, 2, \ldots, 31$.

Neither he, nor Trenchant, of course, used this particular notation. Like Trenchant, Stevin used 10^7 as the base of his system in order to avoid decimal fractions. He never rewrote the tables in his own decimal notation.

In an appendix Stevin describes 'a general rule for finding which is the most profitable of two or more conditions, and by how much it is more profitable than the other'. The rule is to find the present value of each proposed condition in respect to a given rate of interest, the difference between these present values showing by how much one condition is better than the other. This is clearly the net-present-value criterion of choosing between alternative investments. As is to be expected, he applied it only to loans.[1]

After Stevin many other books containing compound-interest tables were published. The first English writer to include them appears to have been Richard Witt in his book *Arithmeticall Questions* (1613).[2]

---

reprinted in *Sarton on the History of Science*, ed. D. Stimson (Cambridge, Mass., Harvard University Press, 1962).

[1] Simon Stevin, *Tafalen van Interest* (Antwerp, Christoffel Plantijn, 1582). The original is reprinted with a facing translation in Struik, *Works of Stevin*, pp. 25–117. The passage quoted is on p. 107 of the translation. Struik's introduction (pp. 13–24) is very informative on the history of interest tables. See also G. W. Smith, 'A Brief History of Interest Calculations', in *Journal of Industrial Engineering*, XVIII (1967) 569–74.

[2] Richard Witt, *Arithmeticall Questions, touching the buying or exchange of annuities* (London, Richard Redmer, 1613) 183 pp.

An understanding of compound interest was one of the preconditions for the development of scientific life-assurance in England in the eighteenth century. Others were the theory of probability and statistics of mortality. The essentials of the mathematical theory of probability were worked out in 1654 in a correspondence between the French mathematicians Pierre de Fermat (1601–65) and Blaise Pascal (1623–62) and were systematised by the Dutch physicist Christianus Huygens (1629–95) in his book *De Ratiociniis in Aleae Ludo* (1657). Shortly afterwards John Graunt (1620–74), a friend of Sir William Petty, published his *Natural and Political Observations made upon the Bills of Mortality* (London, 1662), which contained a rudimentary life-table. The way in which the chances of death could be combined with allowance for compound interest to produce the value of a life annuity was first shown by the Dutch statesman Johann de Witt (1625–72) but his report of 1671 to the States-General was not published and it was in fact the English astronomer Edmond Halley (1656–1742) who, using statistics from bills of mortality for Breslau for the years 1687–91, constructed the first mortality table computed from statistics.[1]

In 1756, James Dodson (1710?–57), F.R.S., 'Accountant and Teacher of the Mathematics', in his unpublished 'First Lecture on Insurances' made the first investigation into the principles of operation of a life assurance business and showed how premiums

[1] F. N. David, *Games, Gods and Gambling* (London, Charles Griffin & Co., 1962) has chapters on Fermat and Pascal, Huygens and Graunt, and also an English translation of the Fermat–Pascal correspondence. The original letters can be found in P. Tannery and C. Henry, *Œuvres de Fermat* (Paris, Gauthier-Villars et fils, 1894) II 288–314; and there is another translation in D. E. Smith, *A Source Book of Mathematics* (New York, McGraw-Hill, 1929) pp. 546–65. Graunt's book was reprinted in 1939 by the Johns Hopkins Press, Baltimore. Halley's paper, 'An estimate of the Degrees of the Mortality of Mankind, drawn from curious tables of the Births and Funerals at the City of Breslaw; with an Attempt to ascertain the Price of Annuities upon Lives', was published in the *Philosophical Transactions of the Royal Society of London*, XVII cxcvi (1693) 596–610, and reprinted by the Johns Hopkins Press in 1942. There are selections from Graunt and Halley in J. R. Newman, *The World of Mathematics*, 4 vols (London, Allen & Unwin, 1960) vol. 3, pt. viii. See also A. Armitage, *Edmond Halley* (London, Nelson, 1966) pp. 127–132.

should be calculated. The general principles he set forth are still valid.¹ His publications include *The Calculator: being correct and necessary Tables for Computation, Adapted to Science, Business, and Pleasure* (London, John Wilcox and James Dodson, 1747); *The Mathematical Repository* (London, John Nourse, 3 vols, 1747-8, 1753, 1755); and the eighteenth and nineteenth editions of Edmund Wingate's *A Plain and Familiar Method for attaining the Knowledge and Practice of Common Arithmetic* (London, 1751 and 1760). All of these books include sections on compound interest and annuities with appropriate tables.²

The operations of the life assurance societies, notably the Equitable Life Assurance Society (founded 1762), gave rise to actuarial science. The first official reference to 'professional actuaries' is to be found in the Poor Law Act of 1819; an Institute of Actuaries was established in England in 1848.³ The first textbook published by the Institute listed and commented upon bond tables prepared by Charles Ingall (1862), Lt-Col. W. H. Oakes (1870) and Herbert Johnson (1881).⁴ The earliest known set of such tables was prepared by the New York banker Joseph M. Price and published in that city in 1843.⁵ The tables can be used to find the yield to maturity of a bond, i.e., that rate of interest which equates the issue or current market price with the stream of future

[1] M. E. Ogborn, *Equitable Assurances* (London, Allen & Unwin, 1962) pp. 30-1.

[2] On Dodson see Augustus de Morgan, 'Some Account of James Dodson, F.R.S.', in *Journal of the Institute of Actuaries*, XIV lxxiii (Oct. 1868) 341-64; Ogborn, *Equitable Assurances*; and V. Snelling, 'Two Respectable Accountants', in *Accountant*, CLI (19 Dec. 1964) 782-3. Dodson was also the author of *The Accountant, or the Method of Book-keeping, Deduced from Clear Principles and Illustrated by a Variety of Examples* (London, J. Nourse, 1750) which is one of the very few early works on book-keeping to deal with accounting for manufacturing operations. Extracts from this book are given in R. S. Edwards, 'Some Notes on the Early Literature and Development of Cost Accounting in Great Britain – II', in *Accountant*, XCVII (Aug. 1937) 226-8.

[3] Ogborn, *Equitable Assurances*, pp. 198, 212; R. C. Simmonds, *The Institute of Actuaries 1848-1948* (London, Institute of Actuaries, 1948).

[4] W. Sutton, *Institute of Actuaries' Text-Book of the Principles of Interest (including Annuities Certain), Life Annuities, and Assurances and their Practical Application. Part 1, Interest (including Annuities Certain)* (London, Layton, 1882) pp. 158, 160.

[5] See Robert M. Soldolfsky, 'A Note on the History of Bond Tables and Stock Valuation Models', in *Journal of Finance*, Mar. 1966.

cash receipts (periodic interest and redemption price). This is clearly a particular application of what was later to be named the marginal efficiency of capital or internal rate of return.

It is difficult to tell how much the writers on engineering and political economy who discussed the criteria for investment decisions owed to the writers mentioned so far. It is certain, however, that Irving Fisher (see pp. 44-5 below) was familiar with the leading actuarial textbook of his day: Ralph Todhunter's *The Institute of Actuaries' Text-Book on Compound Interest and Annuities-Certain* (London, Layton, 1901).[1]

THE CONTRIBUTION OF ENGINEERING ECONOMY

Discounted-cash-flow criteria were not applied to non-financial investments until the late nineteenth century.[2] This was probably due not only to the difficulties of forecasting the relevant cash flows but also to the relatively small size of such investments. It was the coming of the railways which changed this situation. The building of railways entailed a massive capital outlay before any returns were received, so it is not surprising that in the second edition (1887) of his standard work on the location of railways the American civil engineer A. M. Wellington should anticipate some of the ideas of modern capital expenditure analysis. In his chapter on the probable volume of traffic he points out that it is rarely the case that a railway, especially in the United States, is built only for the existing traffic, but also that it is exceedingly dangerous for an average American corporation to look ahead for more than from three to at most ten years for the 'rapidly increasing traffic' which

---

[1] He cites it on pp. 401 and 411 of his *The Nature of Capital and Income* (New York, Macmillan, 1906).

[2] Compound interest and annuity factors have been used in mine valuation at least since the 1st edition of H. D. Hoskold's *Engineer's Valuing Assistant* (London, Longmans, Green, 1877). In the 1890's the shipping firm Harrisons of Liverpool 'were in possession of, and using data which enabled them to apply an early, though admittedly rudimentary, technique for estimating the marginal efficiency of their capital' (F. E. Hyde, *Shipping Enterprise and Management 1830-1939* (Liverpool, Liverpool University Press, 1967) p. 117).

is to justify an increase of present expenditure over what the prospects of the present and the immediate future will justify. He then continues as follows:

> Let us see why this is so. The theory of the subject is simple: In Table 18 is given the present value or present justifiable expenditure to save $1 (or one unit of any other value) at the end of a given period at any given rate of interest; that is to say, the sum which, if placed at compound interest now, will produce $1 at the end of the specified period. This fact given, it logically follows, that if the value of a given betterment for a given immediate traffic be $1, the present value of the same betterment for an equal traffic which is to exist only in the future will be that sum which at compound interest will produce $1 when the assumed traffic comes to exist....
> All this is undeniably correct in theory ... [but] the indications of Table 18 are of value only as fixing a maximum which should never be exceeded....
> ... while it may be taken as a practical certainty that the traffic of any ordinary railway not only will grow, but that it will grow at an average rate of something like 5 to 8 per cent per annum east of the Alleghenies, and 7 to 10 or 15 or even 20 per cent per year west of there, yet ... the rate of this growth of traffic is excessively variable and uncertain – liable to cease altogether at any time for many years....
> For this cause alone it is in general inexpedient to look forward more than at most five years for traffic to justify an increase of immediate expenditure....[1]

A present-value approach was also used by Walter O. Pennell, Equipment and Building Engineer, Southwestern Bell Telephone System, in a paper[2] read to the Engineers' Club, St Louis, Missouri, in April 1914. He discussed the problem of whether to install new machinery or to retain old machinery. In a curiously roundabout manner he first calculates interest and sinking-fund depreciation

---

[1] Wellington, *The Economic Theory of the Location of Railways* (ch. IV. See also pp. 746–7. Wellington's book is discussed by M. B. Scorgie, 'Rate of Return', in *Abacus*, I i (1965) and by R. J. Stephens, 'A Note on an Early Reference to Cost-Volume-Profit Relationships', in *Abacus*, II i (1966).
[2] W. O. Pennell, ' "Present Worth" Calculations in Engineering Studies', in *Journal of the Association of Engineering Societies*, Sept. 1914.

DISCOUNTED CASH FLOW 41

on the initial capital cost and then multiplies by an annuity factor to obtain present worth. This procedure may be shown symbolically as follows:

$$\left(Ci + \frac{C}{s_{n|i}}\right) a_{n|i} = P,$$

where C is the initial capital cost, i the rate of interest, $\frac{1}{s_{n|i}}$ the sinking-fund factor, $a_{n|i}$ the annuity factor and P present worth. But[1]

$$i + \frac{1}{s_{n|i}} = \frac{1}{a_{n|i}}$$

so the left-hand side is simply equal to C, i.e. the present value of C spent now is C! Pennell appears to have confused himself by including in the same calculation both the initial capital cost and the operating expenses.

Pennell also failed to handle properly the abandonment of old machinery. Like many writers he failed to realise the irrelevance of its historical cost.

Another engineering writer, John H. Van Deventer, gave the following advice in an article in the *American Machinist* in 1915: first, estimate the probable saving that an appliance will make; secondly, assign a probable length of life to it; thirdly, estimate what the appliance will cost; fourthly, decide on the minimum rate of return expected. The reader is then referred to a 'Table of Maximum Permissible Investment to Accomplish a Given Saving'. Unfortunately, as Wing has shown, the table does not, despite first appearances to the contrary, make use of compound-interest factors.[2]

---
[1] The proof of the relationship between the sinking-fund factor and the reciprocal of the annuity factor is given in many books, e.g. J. W. Bennett, J. McB. Grant and R. H. Parker, *Topics in Business Finance and Accounting* (Melbourne, Cheshire, 1964) pp. 22–3.

[2] John Van Deventer, 'Jigs and Fixtures in the Small Shop', in *American Machinist*, XLII (1915) 807–9. See also George A. Wing, 'Capital Budgeting, Circa 1915', in *Journal of Finance*, XX (1965) 472–9.

The writings of O. B. Goldman of the Department of Mechanical Engineering of the University of Arizona, and of J. C. F. Fish and E. L. Grant, professors of engineering at Stanford University, show a great advance on the work of Pennell and Van Deventer.

Goldman[1] worked in terms of what he called 'vestances', i.e. the present values of costs. Depreciation vestance he defined as the present worth of investments and reinvestments. If these are expected to go on for ever one obtains the simple formula

$$\frac{C}{1 - (1 + r)^{-n}}$$

which (in a notation not used by Goldman) is equal to

$$\frac{C a_{n|r}^{-1}}{r}$$

where C is the initial cost, r the rate of interest, n the length of life of the initial investment and of each reinvestment, and $a_{n|r}^{-1}$ is the 'capital recovery factor' (a phrase used later by Grant but not by Goldman). If operating costs (a) can also be regarded as constant and perpetual then 'operating vestance' will be $\frac{a}{r}$ and 'total vestance' (V) will be given by the formula

$$V = \frac{C}{1 - (1 + r)^{-n}} + \frac{a}{r}$$

$$= \frac{C a_{n|r}^{-1} + a}{r}$$

If a finite life of mn years is assumed then 'total partial vestance' is given by the formula

$$V'_{mn} = \frac{C[1 - (1 + r)^{-mn}]}{1 - (1 + r)^{-n}} + \frac{a[1 - (1 + r)^{-mn}]}{r}$$

$$= V[1 - (1 + r)^{-mn}]$$

---

[1] O. B. Goldman, *Financial Engineering* (New York, Wiley, 1920, 2nd ed., 1923), especially ch. 2.

DISCOUNTED CASH FLOW 43

Fish and Grant, on the other hand, preferred the 'annual cost method'. Fish explained that in deciding among alternative investments comparison should be made of:
(i) the equivalent uniform annual operation cost (excluding depreciation), which is found by reducing the series of actual annual costs to a convenient date, and distributing the sum of the results uniformly over the whole period;
(ii) annual depreciation cost calculated by the sinking-fund method and taking into account the salvage value;
(iii) interest on capital;
(iv) the equivalent uniform annual income.[1]

Grant[2] explains the use of 'present worth' and 'rate of return on extra investment', but even in the revised fourth edition published in 1964 gives preference to the annual-cost method on the grounds that people understand it more easily and that it is usually easier to compute.[3]

THE CONTRIBUTION OF POLITICAL ECONOMY

It is, however, in the discussions on capital theory by such economists as Marshall in England, Böhm-Bawerk in Austria, Wicksell[4] in Sweden and above all Fisher in the United States that the ultimate source of most of our present ideas on discounted cash flow can be found.

In his *Principles of Economics* Marshall wrote of the accumulation of past and the discounting of future outlays and receipts. The balance of efforts and satisfactions involved in an investment may be made up to any day that is found convenient, but whatever day is chosen every effort or satisfaction which dates from a time

---

[1] J. C. L. Fish, *Engineering Economics* (New York, McGraw-Hill, 1915, 2nd ed. 1923) chs II and IV.
[2] E. L. Grant, *Principles of Engineering Economy* (New York, Ronald, 1930, 2nd ed., 1938, 3rd ed., 1950, 4th ed. (with W. G. Ireson) 1960).
[3] Grant and Ireson, *Principles of Engineering Economy* (1964) p. 103.
[4] K. Wicksell, *Value Capital and Rent* (London, Allen & Unwin, 1954) pt. II (German original published in 1893); and *Lectures on Political Economy*, vol. I, pt. II, ch. 2 (London, Routledge, 1934) (Swedish original published in 1901).

anterior to that day must have compound interest for the interval accumulated upon it; and every element which dates from a time posterior to that day must have compound interest for the interval discounted from it. Allowance should be made for the risk of failure. Difficulties may arise from changes in the general purchasing power of money. An alert businessman will push investment of capital in his business in each direction until what appears in his judgement to be the margin of profitableness has been reached, i.e. until there seems to him no good reason for thinking that the gains resulting from any further investment in that particular direction would compensate him for his outlay.[1]

Böhm-Bawerk also had a net-present-value approach. He gives as an example the problem of whether to buy a house offered for the payment of twenty annual instalments of 1000 florins each. The present value of the house should not, he says, be compared with the rate of sacrifice currently experienced (i.e. the first instalment only) but with the value of the entire twenty instalments entered at their present value.[2]

Fisher's work clearly owes something not only to his economist predecessors such as Böhm-Bawerk but also to the writers on actuarial science and finance already mentioned. This said, it is important to stress how far he was in advance of them and indeed of most of his *successors* until the 1950's.

His most important work in this field was *The Rate of Interest* first published in 1907 and extensively revised and reissued as *The Theory of Interest* in 1930. In these books he sets out four ways of choosing between investment options and claims that they all give the same result. Out of all eligible options one should select (i) the one which has the maximum present value, reckoned at the market rate of interest (the principle of maximum present value); (ii) the one whose advantages (returns) over any other outweigh, in present value, its disadvantages (costs), when both returns and

[1] A. Marshall, *Principles of Economics*, 2 vols (London, Macmillan for the Royal Economic Society, 9th (variorum) ed., 1961) I 352–6, II 368–71. The passage paraphrased first appears in the 5th ed., 1907.
[2] A. v. Böhm-Bawerk, *Recent Literature on Interest (1884–1899)* (New York, Macmillan, 1903) p. 36 n. English translation by W. A. Scott and S. Feilbogen.

costs are discounted at the market rate of interest (the principle of comparative advantage); (iii) the one which, compared with any other option, yields a 'rate of return on sacrifice' or 'rate of return over cost' greater than the rate of interest (the principle of return over cost); or (iv) where options differ by continuous gradations, the one the difference of which from its nearest rival gives a rate of return over cost equal to the rate of interest (such a rate is called the *marginal* rate of return over cost).

These criteria are illustrated by examples of the alternative use of land. One example uses the following figures:

	Annual Value of Uses for Forestry	Farming	Difference in Favour of Forestry
	$	$	$
1st year	000	100	−100
2nd year	210	100	+110
3rd year and each subsequent year	100	100	000

At a market rate of interest of 9 per cent the forestry use should be preferred because it has the greater present value ($1112 as against $1111 for farming) and because the rate of return over cost, 10 per cent, is greater than the market rate. The rate of return over cost is computed from the difference column by solving for r in the equation $100 = 110/(1+r)$. At a market rate of interest of 10 per cent the two uses are equal, both having a present value of $1000 and the rate of return over cost being equal to the market rate of interest. At a market rate of 11 per cent the farming use will be preferred since its present value is $909 as against $908 for forestry, and since the rate of return over cost (10 per cent) is less than the market rate.[1]

Fisher's rate of return over cost is *not* the same as the internal rate of return or marginal efficiency of capital discussed by Boulding, Samuelson and Keynes in the 1930's. This refers to a single

[1] I. Fisher, *The Rate of Interest* (New York, Macmillan, 1907) ch. 8; *The Theory of Interest* (New York, Macmillan, 1930) ch. 7.

investment only. Boulding pointed out that the internal rate of return could be calculated from the equation

$$V_0 = \frac{x_1}{(1+i)} + \frac{x_2}{(1+i)^2} + \cdots \frac{x_n}{(1+i)^n}$$

where V_0 is the value of the enterprise, $i =$ the internal rate of return, $n =$ the number of periods and $x_1, x_2, \ldots, x_n =$ a series of known net revenues (positive or negative). He noted that the solution was not mathematically a simple one but he thought that in most practical cases a single solution could be found. He did not regard multiple rates of return as of much economic significance. In the context of the single investment which he was considering he was probably right.[1]

In *The General Theory* Keynes defined the 'marginal efficiency of capital' of an asset as being equal to that rate of discount which would make the present value of the returns expected from the asset during its life just equal to its current supply price and claimed that this was identical with Fisher's rate of return over cost.[2] He correctly quoted Fisher as stating that 'the rate of return over cost is always that rate which, employed in computing the present worth of all the costs and the present worth of all the returns, will make these two equal'. But he omitted the sentences which follow:

Or, as a mathematician would prefer to put it, the rate which, employed in computing the present worth of the whole series of differences between the two income streams (some differences being positive and others negative) will make the total zero.

If the rate, so computed, were taken for every possible pair of income streams compared as to their advantages and disadvantages, it would authentically decide in each case which of the pair is to be preferred. That one which compared with the other shows a rate of return on

---

[1] K. E. Boulding, 'The Theory of a Single Investment', in *Quarterly Journal of Economics*, XLIX (May 1935); 'Time and Investment', in *Economica*, May 1936; C. A. Wright, 'A Note on "Time and Investment" ', in *Economica*, Nov. 1936; K. E. Boulding, ' "Time and Investment", A Reply', in *Economica*, Nov. 1936.

[2] J. M. Keynes, *The General Theory of Employment, Interest and Money* (London, Macmillan, 1936) pp. 140-1.

sacrifice greater than the rate of interest would be preferred and the other rejected. By such preferences and rejections the individual would be led to a final *margin* of choice of the best option. This contrasted with its nearest rival would show a marginal rate of return over cost equal to the market rate of interest.[1]

When, at last, in the 1950's discounted-cash-flow methods started to become familiar it was Keynes's misinterpretation which became best-known.

The contributions made by Boulding and Keynes were discussed by Samuelson in the *Quarterly Journal of Economics* in 1937. He noted the essential equivalence of his own internal rate of interest, Boulding's internal rate of return and Keynes's marginal efficiency of capital and pointed out quite clearly the possibility of no rate of return or of multiple rates. He rejected Boulding's view that it is the internal rate of return which a perfectly rational and foreseeing investor should maximise and claimed that at least under ideal conditions the proper principle was clear and was an old one in the literature of the subject:

Given an interest rate at which all can lend or borrow [r^0] *each entrepreneur will select that value of the variable under his control which maximises the present value of the investment account, the present value being computed by capitalization of the income stream at the market rate of interest. This follows from the fact that under our ideal conditions, the investment account necessarily has a market value equal to the capitalized value, and is equivalent to an equal money sum, and a larger initial sum of money is always to be preferred to a smaller one.*[2]

J. B. Williams' book, *The Theory of Investment Value* (1938) was very much concerned with present values – one chapter was entitled 'Evaluation by the Rule of Present Worth' – but in the

[1] Fisher, *Theory of Interest*, pp. 168–9. Keynes's error was first pointed out by A. A. Alchian in his article 'The Rate of Interest, Fisher's Rate of Return over Cost and Keynes' Internal Rate of Return', in *American Economic Review*, Dec. 1955, reprinted in *The Management of Corporate Capital*, ed. E. Solomon (New York, Free Press of Glencoe, 1959).
[2] P. A. Samuelson, 'Some Aspects of the Pure Theory of Capital', in *Quarterly Journal of Economics*, LI (May 1937), reprinted in *The Collected Scientific Papers of Paul A. Samuelson*, ed. J. E. Stiglitz (Cambridge, Mass., M.I.T. Press, 1966) I.

context of financial assets and liabilities. It has an important place in the history of the concept of the cost of capital, which we have excluded from discussion in this chapter.

An early use of the present-value criterion was made by the South African Mining Industry Commission of 1907-8 in an attempt to measure the return on capital invested in the Witwatersrand gold industry. In later investigations (1923, 1935, 1967) of the same problem by Lehfeldt and Frankel the internal-rate-of-return criterion was used. It is interesting to note that the use of these criteria was influenced by the fact that conventional accounting rates of return are difficult to calculate for companies which do not provide for depreciation on wasting assets.[1]

There are very few references to making investment decisions in the accounting literature of the 1930's. The net-present-value method, however, was clearly described by the economist R. H. Coase in a series of articles in the *Accountant* in 1938.[2] His articles appear to have had very little impact on accounting theory and even less on accounting practice, although after being reprinted in 1952 they were quite widely used in university accounting courses.

On the actual practice of investment in the late 1930's we have some evidence from surveys carried out at Oxford and Harvard on the significance of changes in rates of interest on influencing the decisions of savers and borrowers. Sir Hubert Henderson of the Oxford Economists' Research Group reported in 1938 that frequently in response to the Group's questions 'the methods of calculation actually employed in weighing projects of capital expenditure were precisely explained; and these were such as to

[1] See R. A. Lehfeldt, 'Return to Capital Invested in the Witwatersrand', in *Journal of the Chemical, Metallurgical and Mining Society of South Africa*, Jan. 1923; S. H. Frankel, 'Return to Capital Invested in the Witwatersrand Gold-Mining Industry, 1887-1932', in *Economic Journal*, Mar. 1935, and his books *Capital Investment in Africa* (Oxford University Press, 1938) and *Investment and the Return to Equity Capital in the South African Gold Mining Industry 1887-1965* (Oxford, Basil Blackwell, 1967).
I am indebted to Professor L. H. Samuels of the University of Witwatersrand for these references.
[2] R. H. Coase, 'Business Organisation and the Accountant', in *Accountant*, 1 Oct.-17 Dec. 1938, reprinted in Solomons, *Studies in Costing*.

DISCOUNTED CASH FLOW 49

disregard altogether variations in interest rates'. In a survey based on cases collected by the Harvard Business School, J. F. Ebersole reported that there was a strong presumption that the interest rate was seldom considered as a factor in the entrepreneurial decisions of business to expand or contract, and that it was a controlling factor in a negligible number of instances.[1] As late as 1951 Gort reported that discounting methods were not used in the American electric power industry.[2]

DISCOUNTED CASH FLOW IN THE 1950'S AND 1960'S

It was not until the 1950's that interest in discounted cash flow methods began to quicken. One of the early popularisers was the managerial economist Joel Dean. In the early 1950's he studied the capital-expenditure methods of some fifty 'well-managed' large companies. He found that there was widespread failure to measure the investment worth of individual proposals directly, a lack of defensible objective standards of an acceptable investment and an inadequate understanding of the economic content of the concepts used. The companies were still forced to play by ear to a distressing extent.[3] The most commonly used criteria in his experience were degree of necessity or postponability; payback period ('unquestionably the most widely used measure of investment worth'); and 'rate of return'. The calculation of the rate of return was

[1] H. D. Henderson, 'The Significance of the Rate of Interest', in *Oxford Economic Papers*, I (1938) 8–9; reprinted in *Oxford Studies in the Price Mechanism*, ed. T. Wilson and P. W. S. Andrews (Oxford, Clarendon Press, 1951) p. 24; J. F. Ebersole, 'The Influence of Interest Rates upon Entrepreneurial Decisions in Business – A Case Study', in *Harvard Business Review*, XVII i (1938). See also Ruth P. Mack, *The Flow of Business Funds and Consumer Purchasing Power* (New York, Columbia University Press, 1941) ch. 8, especially pp. 265–7. For a summary of these and other empirical findings on the influence of interest rates see J. R. Meyer and E. Kuh, *The Investment Decision* (Cambridge, Mass., Harvard University Press, 1957) pp. 25–6.

[2] M. Gort, 'The Planning of Investment: A Study of Capital Budgeting in the Electric-Power Industry', in *Journal of Business*, XXIV (1951) p. 194.

[3] J. Dean, 'Measuring the Productivity of Capital', in *Harvard Business Review*, Jan.-Feb. 1954; reprinted in Solomon, *Management of Corporate Capital*, and in Baxter and Davidson, *Studies in Accounting Theory*.

based either on financial accounting procedures or on discounted cash flow methods. Use of the latter gives, of course, the internal-rate-of-return rule and it is this approach which was strongly recommended by Dean under the name 'profitability yield'.[1]

A number of writers, however, were already challenging the internal-rate-of-return approach, e.g. F. and V. Lutz in their *Theory of Investment of the Firm*.[2] Three problems in particular were discussed: choosing between mutually exclusive investments; the possibility of multiple rates of return; and capital rationing.

Keynes's misinterpretation of Fisher's rate of return over cost was pointed out in 1955 by Alchian,[3] who showed that the

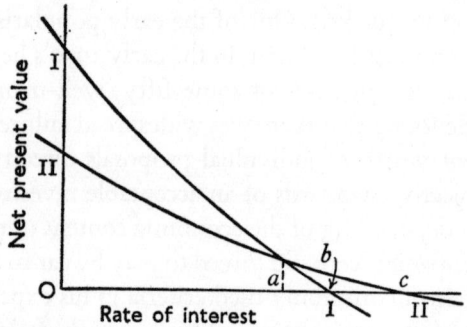

Fig. 3.1 Net Present Value Curves of Mutually Exclusive Investments

ranking of mutually exclusive investments by the Keynesian internal rate of return is not consistent with the maximising of net present wealth. This can be illustrated by a diagram (see Fig. 3.1; Alchian in fact measured his rate of interest on a log scale).

[1] See also his books *Capital Budgeting* (New York, Columbia University Press, 1951) and *Managerial Economics* (Englewood Cliffs, N.J., Prentice-Hall, 1951) ch. 10.
[2] F. and V. Lutz, *The Theory of Investment of the Firm* (Princeton, N.J., Princeton University Press, 1951) ch. 2.
[3] A. A. Alchian, 'The Rate of Interest, Fisher's Rate of Return over Cost and Keynes' Internal Rate of Return', in *American Economic Review*, Dec. 1955; reprinted in Solomon, *Management of Corporate Capital*.

I–I and *II–II* are the net-present-value curves of two mutually exclusive investments. By the internal-rate-of-return criterion investment *II* is always preferable since its rate of return is *Oc* as against *Ob* for investment *I*. By the net-present-value criterion, however, investment *I* is preferable if the cost of capital is less than *Oa*. *Oa* itself is the Fisherian rate of return over cost.

Writing three years later Hirshleifer[1] provided a numerical example to illustrate the same point. Assume that the cash flows of the two investments are as follows:

	End of Period		
	0	1	2
I	−1	0	4
II	−1	2	1

The internal rate of return of investment *I* is 100 per cent; of investment *II* 141·4 per cent. The present value of *I* is greater than that of *II* for all rates of interest up to 50 per cent. Suppose that at a rate less than this (say 10 per cent) we adopt investment *I*. Next we borrow 3 from period 2 and credit period 1 with $3/1 \cdot 1 = 2 \cdot 73$. We now have:

End of Period		
0	1	2
−1	2·73	1

Throwing away 0·73 in the first period leaves us with:

End of Period		
0	1	2
−1	2	1

which is, of course, investment *II*. The fact that we can convert investment *I* to investment *II* by throwing away wealth shows that at interest rates less than that at the point of intersection of the two net-present-value curves investment *I* is preferable to investment *II*.

---

[1] J. Hirshleifer, 'On the Theory of Optimal Investment Decision', in *Journal of Political Economy*, Aug. 1958 (reprinted in Solomon, *Management of Corporate Capital*), footnote 39.

Much attention was given to the problem of multiple rates of return. Lorie and Savage[1] pointed out that when considering a single investment there is no conflict between the internal-rate-of-return and net-present-value rules so long as the net present value

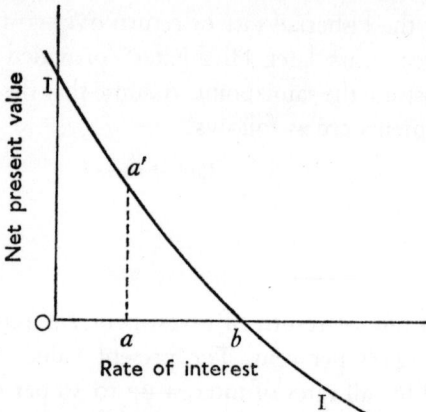

Fig. 3.2 Net Present Value Curve of a Single Investment

is a steadily decreasing function of the firm's cost of capital. In Fig. 3.2, I–I indicates the present value of an investment at different rates of interest; Oa is the firm's cost of capital; Ob is the internal rate of return of the investment; and aa' is the present value of the investment at the firm's cost of capital. It is clear from the diagram that any investment which has a positive present value at the firm's cost of capital will also have an internal rate of return greater than the cost of capital.

A conflict between the two criteria will occur, however, even in the single-investment case, if the net-present-value curve is as shown in Fig. 3.3 (this may occur if some of the anticipated net receipts are negative).

This is the problem of multiple rates of return. The internal rate of return of the proposed investment is both Ob and Oc. There is,

[1] J. H. Lorie and L. J. Savage, 'Three Problems in Rationing Capital', in *Journal of Business*, Oct. 1955, reprinted in Solomon, *Management of Corporate Capital*.

however, only one net present value at the cost of capital Oa, viz. aa'.

This problem, whose existence, it will be remembered, was referred to by Boulding and Samuelson in the 1930's, was further

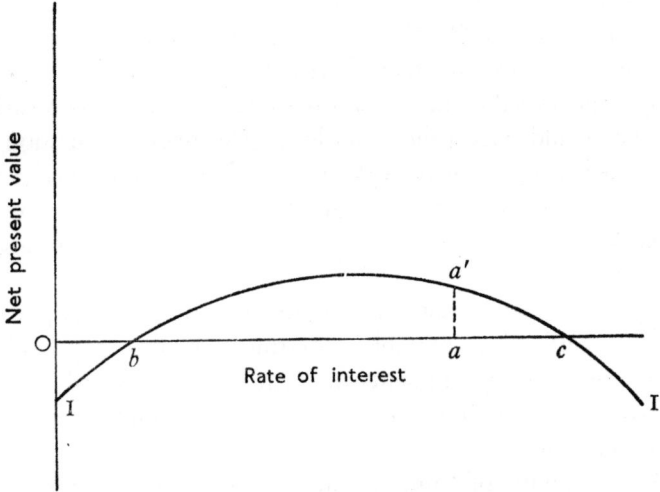

Fig. 3.3 Multiple Rates of Return

discussed by Solomon and Renshaw[1] with reference to the replacement of a pump in an oil well by a larger pump. The example can be summarised as follows:

	Cash Flows		
	A	B	C
	Investment	No	Incremental Cash Flow
Time	in a	Additional	due to Investment
Period	Larger Pump	Investment	in Larger Pump
t_0	−1,600	0	−1,600
t_1	20,000	10,000	10,000
t_2	0	10,000	−10,000

[1] E. Solomon, 'The Arithmetic of Capital-Budgeting Decisions', in *Journal of Business*, Apr. 1956; E. Renshaw, 'A Note on the Arithmetic of Capital Budgeting Decisions', in *Journal of Business*, July 1957; both reprinted in Solomon, *Management of Corporate Capital*.

The internal rate of return of A is 1150 per cent; the internal rate of return of B is infinite. The Fisherian rate of return over cost of the incremental cash flows is *both* 25 per cent and 40 per cent. Between these two rates the net present value is positive, i.e. alternative A has a higher net present value than alternative B and hence, according to Renshaw, is the preferred alternative. Solomon argued, however, that all that the installation of a larger pump achieves is that the investor receives $10,000 one year earlier than he would have otherwise done. The relevant question is: how much is this worth to the investor? If he could invest the $10,000 at, say, 23 per cent, then by investing $1600 now he would have $2300 more at t_2, which is a rate of return of about 20 per cent.[1]

Hirshleifer pointed out that not only are multiple rates possible but that 'perfectly respectable' investment options may have *no* real internal rates, the present-value equation having only imaginary roots, i.e. at no point does the net-present-value curve cut the horizontal axis.[2]

The possibility of multiple rates of return was pointed out independently by the Australian economists Pitchford and Hagger in a note in the September 1958 *Economic Journal*.[3] In the discussion that followed, the point was made that if an investment can be terminated at any point it is possible to avoid multiple yields.[4] The Pitchford and Hagger example was as follows:

End of Period					
0	1	2	3	4	5
−2·2	15	−25	0	0	30

[1] The use of explicit reinvestment rates was also recommended by R. H. Baldwin in 'How to Assess Investment Proposals', in *Harvard Business Review*, May-June 1959.

[2] J. Hirshleifer, in *Journal of Political Economy*, Aug. 1958.

[3] J. D. Pitchford and A. J. Hagger, 'A Note on the Marginal Efficiency of Capital', in *Economic Journal*, LVIII (1958) 597–600.

[4] C. S. Soper, 'The Marginal Efficiency of Capital: A Further Note', in *Economic Journal*, LIX (1959) 174–7; P. H. Karmel, 'The Marginal Efficiency of Capital', in *Economic Record*, XXXV (1959) 429–34; J. F. Wright, 'The Marginal Efficiency of Capital', in *Economic Journal*, LIX (1959) 813–16. The problem of multiple rates was

This rather curious project has three internal rates of return: 76 per cent, 120 per cent and 300 per cent. If it is terminated at the end of the first period, however, it has only one rate of return: 580 per cent.

Lorie and Savage posed, but failed to find a satisfactory answer to, the capital-rationing problem: given a fixed sum for capital investment, what group of investment projects should be undertaken?[1] The necessity of a mathematical-programming approach was first shown by Weingartner.[2]

There is some evidence of a growing practical application of discounted cash flow methods in the 1950's – at least in the United States. Eisner's study *Determinants of Capital Expenditures* (1956) tells us something of the first half of the decade:

Consideration of the various formal costs and earnings criteria reportedly used by business firms in deciding upon capital expenditures led into something of a wilderness where method was difficult to find. Rules of thumb appeared unduly crude and frequently internally inconsistent. Under probing questioning, responsible officials indicated ignorance as to the specific nature of the calculations underlying their rules or they advised sagely that 'judgment' was more important than rules.

Payback period and rates of return based on financial accounting procedures were used by many firms. Eisner found the handling of depreciation charges 'downright offensive to one nurtured in the concepts of the marginal efficiency of investment'.[3] In his book *Capital Expenditure Decisions: how they are made in large corporations* (1961) Istvan reported that of the forty-eight firms studied by him

---

also discussed in J. B. Weaver, 'False and Multiple Solutions by the Discounted Cash Flow Method for Determining Interest Rate of Return', in *Engineering Economist*, III (Spring 1958) 1–31.

[1] Lorie and Savage (Solomon reprint) pp. 58–61, 64–5.

[2] H. M. Weingartner, *Mathematical Programming and the Analysis of Capital Budgeting Problems* (Chicago, Markham Publishing Co., 1967) (1st ed. published by Prentice-Hall in 1963).

[3] R. Eisner, *Determinants of Capital Expenditures* (Urbana, Illinois, Bureau of Economic and Business Research, University of Illinois, 1956) pp. 29–30. See also M. D. Brockie and A. L. Grey, Jr, 'The Marginal Efficiency of Capital and Investment Programming', in *Economic Journal*, LXVI (Dec. 1956) 662–75.

in the second half of the decade five used some form of discounted-cash-flow criterion as a primary measure and nine used it in a supplementary manner. 'Accounting' rate of return and payback period were the most popular methods.[1]

Discounted-cash-flow methods appear to have had little practical impact in the United Kingdom before the 1960's. Even in the early 1960's the surveys by Hart and Prussman, by Lawson, by Neild for the National Institute of Economic and Social Research, and by Williams and Scott for the Centre for Business Research of the University of Manchester showed that D.C.F. was used by only a small minority of firms.[2] On the other hand a number of large organisations, such as the Central Electricity Generating Board and Courtaulds, have adopted some form of D.C.F. criterion.[3] The recent writings of Alfred and Evans of Courtaulds and of Merrett and Sykes[4] have been very influential in spreading the use of D.C.F. techniques in the United Kingdom. The

---

[1] D. F. Istvan, *Capital Expenditure Decisions: how they are made in large corporations* (Bureau of Business Research, Graduate School of Business, Indiana University, 1961) p. 96. Eisner's and Istvan's findings are summarised in Olle Renck 'Empirical Studies of Investment Behaviour', in *Management International*, IV (1964) 70–80, which also gives details of similar studies made in Germany, Sweden, the United Kingdom, the Netherlands and Norway.

[2] H. Hart and D. F. Prussman, *A Report of a Survey of Management Accounting Techniques in the S.E. Hants Coastal Region* (Dept of Commerce and Accountancy, University of Southampton, Dec. 1963) (mimeographed) p. 12; G. H. Lawson, 'Criteria to be Observed in Judging a Capital Project', in *Accountants' Journal* (U.K.), May 1964, pp. 222–6 and June 1964, pp. 267–78; R. R. Neild, 'Replacement Policy', in *National Institute Economic Review*, Nov. 1964; B. R. Williams and W. P. Scott, *Investment Proposals and Decisions* (London, Allen & Unwin, 1965). See also D. C. Corner and A. Williams, 'The Sensitivity of Business to Initial and Investment Allowances', in *Economica*, XXXII (Feb. 1965) Table 1, p. 36.

[3] F. H. S. Brown and R. S. Edwards, 'The Replacement of Obsolescent Plant', in *Economica*, Aug. 1961, pp. 297–302; A. M. Alfred, *Discounted Cash Flow and Corporate Planning* (Woolwich Economic Paper no. 3, 1964); A. M. Alfred and J. B. Evans, *Appraisal of Investment Projects by Discounted Cash Flow* (London, Chapman & Hall, 1965, 2nd ed., 1967); A. M. Alfred, 'Decision Taken', *Management Decision*, Summer 1967, pp. 43–6.

[4] A. J. Merrett and A. Sykes, *The Finance and Analysis of Capital Projects* (London, Longmans, 1963) and *Capital Budgeting and Company Finance* (London, Longmans, 1966).

National Economic Development Council has also been quite active in this field.[1]

Why has it taken so long for the application of discounted-cash-flow criteria to non-financial investments to gain acceptance in practice? The essential clue is surely to be found in the one group so conspicuously absent from this chapter – accountants. It is true that Pacioli in the fifteenth century, Stevin in the sixteenth century and Dodson in the eighteenth century wrote on compound interest and actuarial problems as well as on accounting, but the accounting profession as it developed in the nineteenth century concerned itself much more with historical recording than with decision-making. Nevertheless it was accountants in their rôle as financial experts who were in most cases consulted on capital-expenditure decisions. Since their education did not include much economic theory they naturally turned either to rates of return based on the traditional financial statements or to such simple and conservative techniques as the payback period. The relatively few economists who took an interest in accounting and who made recommendations based on economic theory were ignored. Such was the fate of R. H. Coase's excellent series of articles in the *Accountant* in 1938.[2]

It was not until the 1950's that economists began to play an important part as advisers in business. In the same decade accountants became more acquainted with economic ideas. In this new climate – whose coming in the United Kingdom was perhaps delayed a decade compared with the U.S.A. – the practical use of discounted-cash-flow criteria became not only possible but, we may say with the advantage of hindsight, inevitable.

SUMMARY

Discounted cash flow has its roots in compound interest, actuarial science, engineering economy and capital theory. The net-present-value approach was applied to financial investments by Simon

[1] National Economic Development Council, *Investment Appraisal* (London H.M.S.O., 1965, 2nd ed., 1967).
[2] See p. 48, n. 2 above.

Stevin of Bruges as early as 1582. Bond tables incorporating the equivalent of the internal rate of return were in use by the second half of the nineteenth century, by which time economists and engineers were beginning to discuss the application of discounting to non-financial investments. It was not until the 1950's, however, that interest in the use of D.C.F. techniques began to quicken and it is only in the 1960's that this use has become at all widespread. It is suggested that the bias towards historical recording in the education and training of accountants may have been responsible for this long delay.

4 The Origins of the Break-Even Chart

FIXED AND VARIABLE COSTS

The distinction between costs which are fixed over a given range of production and those which are variable is fundamental to accounting for decision-making. In this chapter we trace the origins of the simple mathematical model based upon this distinction usually known as the break-even chart.

The break-even chart is a relatively new technique, in comparison, say, with the antiquity of double-entry book-keeping. This is because the distinction between fixed and variable costs was of very little practical importance until the Industrial Revolution. Professor de Roover, for example, has constructed an operating statement for the years 1556–8 of Francesco di Guiliano di Raffaello de' Medici & Co., a firm of cloth-manufacturers in Florence. This shows overhead charges of about 10 per cent on sales. De Roover comments:

> Industrial enterprises were then highly flexible units and could adapt themselves readily to a slacker demand by simply curtailing their volume of production. Each curtailment engendered unemployment, but it did not necessarily turn profits into losses, as would be the case in a modern industrial concern with top-heavy overhead.[1]

By the nineteenth century this had ceased to be true in many British industries, notably textiles, iron-manufacturing and railway transport, but a clear distinction between the fixed and variable costs of the individual firm was not made until the 1830's when Charles Babbage gave the example of a manufacturer who having invested a large capital in machinery 'quickly perceived

[1] R. de Roover, 'A Florentine Firm of Cloth Manufacturers', in *Speculum*, XVI (1941) 26.

that with the same expense of fixed capital, and a small addition to his circulating capital, he could work the machine for twenty-four hours instead of eight'.[1] Two years later the economist Robert Torrens pointed out that additional quantities of raw materials could often be worked up 'without incurring an additional expense for buildings and machinery'.[2]

In 1850 Dionysius Lardner of University College, London, dealt with the matter at greater length in his book on railway economics. The cost of production, he noted, 'may always be regarded as consisting of two parts, one of which is quite independent of the number of articles produced, and being, therefore, equally divided among them, will render one element of their price precisely in the inverse ratio of the number; but still there will be another component, which depending on the direct application of manual or other labour, and on the immediate consumption of raw material, will be in the direct ratio of the number of articles produced'.[3] The economist Nassau Senior noted in 1862 that there were 'certain expenses upon a mill which go on in the same proportion whether the mill be running short or full time, as for instance, rent, rates and taxes, insurance against fire, wages of several permanent servants, deterioration of machinery, with various other charges upon a manufacturing establishment, the proportion of which to profits increases as the production decreases'.[4]

Garcke and Fells (respectively an engineer and an accountant) in their book *Factory Accounts* (1887) recognised that 'establishment

[1] Charles Babbage, *On the Economy of Machinery and Manufactures* (London, Charles Knight, 1832) p. 174.
[2] R. Torrens, *On Wages and Combination* (London, Longman, Rees, Orme, Brown, Green, & Longman, 1834) p. 64.
[3] D. Lardner, *Railway Economy* (London, Taylor, Walton & Maberly, 1850) pp. 216-17. This fascinating book also contains the first use of the word 'derailment' in English and such 'Plain Rules for Railway Travellers' as 'beware of yielding to the sudden impulse to spring from the carriage to recover your hat which has blown off'.
[4] Report of Inspector of Factories for 31 Oct. 1862, p. 19, cited by K. Marx, *Capital* (London, Allen & Unwin, 1938) 1 404 (English translation of the 3rd German edition).

expenses', which they defined as the general expenses which could not be *directly* charged to any particular process or branch of a business, 'do not vary proportionately with the volume of business. A large increase in the value of orders received would not necessitate a like augmentation of the office staff, nor would a sudden and serious falling off in trade enable a firm to effect an immediate or proportionate reduction of general expenditure.' They regarded establishment expenses as being, in the aggregate, more or less constant whilst the manufacturing costs fluctuated with the cost of labour and the price of material.[1]

Marshall in his *Principles of Economics* (1890) distinguished between *prime cost*, the expenses which a businessman incurs directly and specially for the production of a commodity, and *supplementary cost*, a share of the general expenses of the business. Included in prime cost were 'the (money) cost of the raw material used in making the commodity and the wages of that part of the labour spent on it which is paid by the day or the week'. The salaries of 'the upper employés' should be excluded from the prime cost, 'partly because the time which they have devoted specially to producing the commodity cannot always be easily ascertained, and partly because the charges to which the business is put on account of their salaries cannot be adapted quickly to changes in the amount of work there is for them to do'. Marshall noted that prime cost is, leaving aside the possibility of spoiling the market, normally the lowest price at which it would be worth while to accept an order.[2]

In the United States much the same points were made by A. T. Hadley in 1896:

In manufactures . . . the units of capital are much larger. Each producer can extend his output with a gain rather than a loss in economy. If he can increase his sales, there will be only a slight increase – perhaps none at all – in the expense for wages and materials and a decided decrease in

---

[1] E. Garcke and J. M. Fells, *Factory Accounts* (London, Crosby Lockwood, 1887) p. 74.
[2] A. Marshall, *Principles of Economics* (London, Macmillan, 1890) pp. 519–20.

the share of the charges on fixed capital which each unit of product must pay.[1]

THE CONTRIBUTION OF HENRY HESS

The time was thus ripe for the break-even chart and the first article on the subject in fact appeared in the *Engineering Magazine* in December 1903.[2] Its author was Henry Hess (1864–1922), a German-born member of the American Society of Mechanical Engineers.

In his article he pointed out that some costs are fixed and some are 'variable with the intensity of the output'. He defined Total Fixed Costs as including all those items that are to be provided to put the plant in readiness and Total Variable Costs per Productive Hour as including all the remaining elements that may be reduced to a ratio with the productive hours. In a diagram (Fig. 4.1 below) labelled 'Costs, Receipts, and Profits' he showed the graphical relationship between these and Total Net Receipts. He condemned the usual practice of considering all general expenses as directly proportional to labour cost since this led to wrong conclusions 'that may, when production is low, give the impression of a margin of profit when actually there is a loss'.

In another diagram (Fig. 4.2) Hess added curves for Total Capital Employed, Total Profits as percentage of Capital Employed, percentage Dividends on Capital Employed and Price per Hour or per Pound to balance costs. This last is, of course, the average-cost curve drawn as a rectangular hyperbola. His diagram did, he claimed, illustrate in a forcible manner the decided advantage of an active output in improving the dividend. He is careful to point out, however, that the same increase cannot go on indefinitely as there comes a point when the production of a larger output is possible only by the provision of enlarged facilities and a corresponding increase in capital employed.

---

[1] A. T. Hadley, *Economics*, (New York, G. P. Putnam's Sons, 1896), p. 152.
[2] Henry Hess, 'Manufacturing: Capital, Costs, Profits and Dividends', in *Engineering Magazine*, XXVI (1903) 367–79.

THE ORIGINS OF THE BREAK-EVEN CHART 63

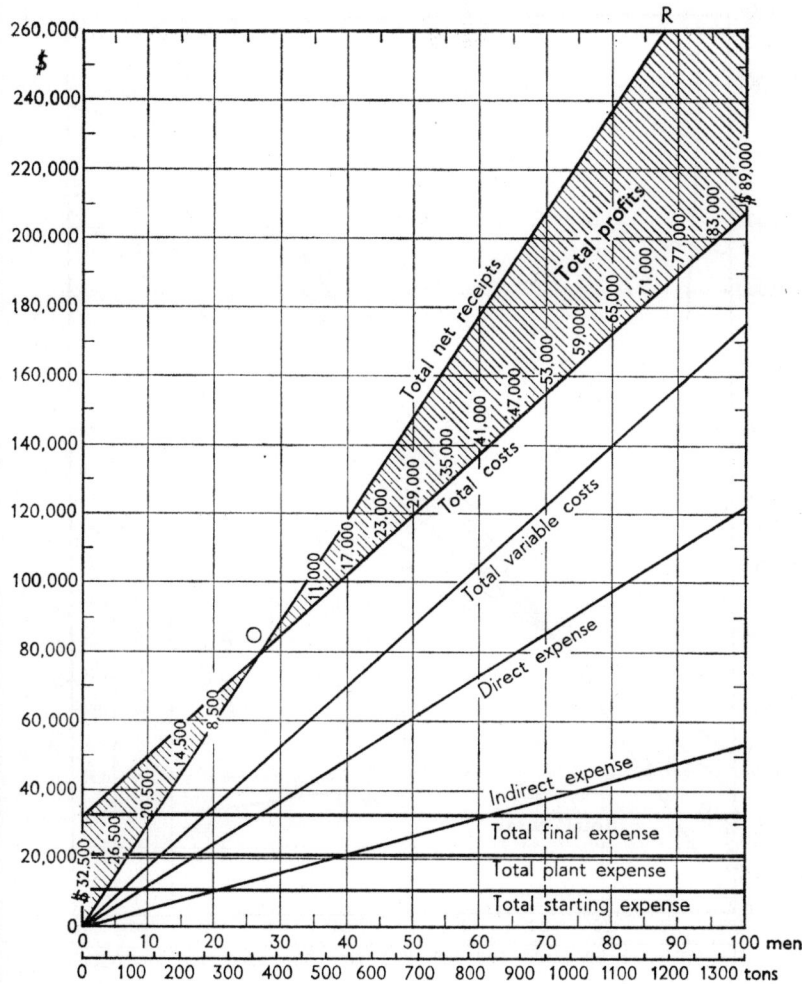

Fig. 4.1 Costs, Receipts, and Profits (Henry Hess, 1903)

Hess also emphasised the importance of his chart for *control*:

All that has been said so far applies to the forecasting of the results of an existing business or of one to be established, but the methods are useful also for following up costs in detail and for pointing out the essential relation and importance of the various elements of costs and so

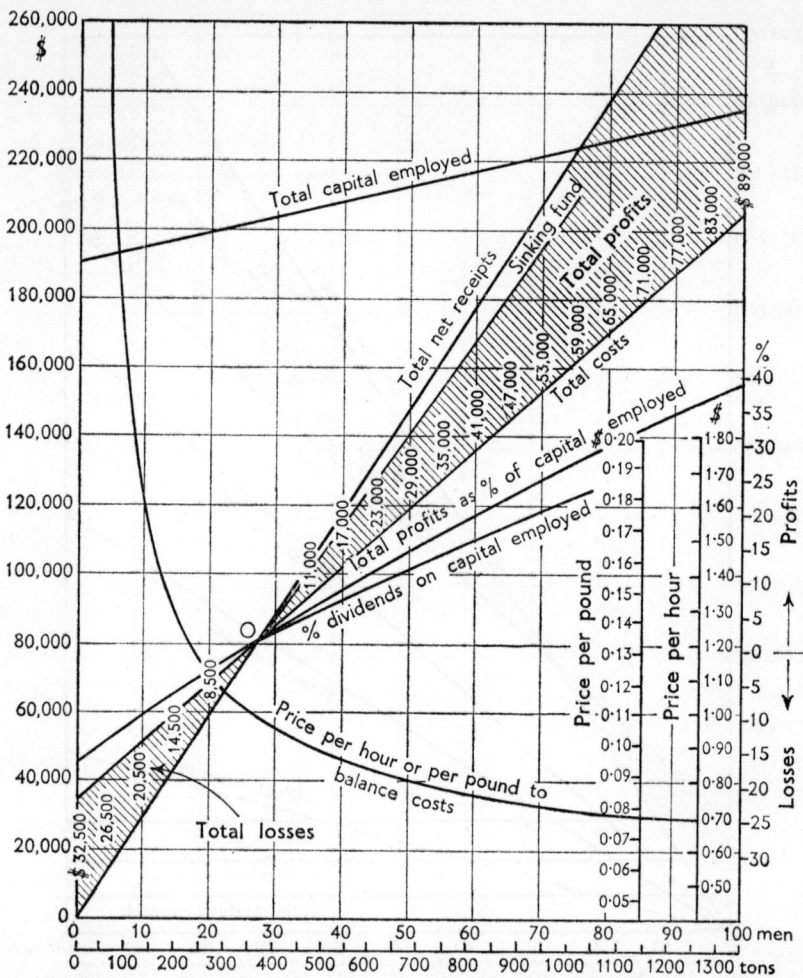

Fig. 4.2 Capital, Profit, and Dividends (Henry Hess, 1903)

showing when effort must be applied to bring about those economies that count most.

Forecasting is quite useful, but far more important is it to make sure that results agree materially with such forecasts and to find the causes for whatever divergencies there may be. For this purpose the lines laid down in the diagrams may be considered as scales by which actual results are measured. ... Since with lines as here laid down the costs are entered vertically over the output weight or number of productive men employed, the influence of fluctuation [of output] is considered and eliminated as a disturbing factor in the costs.

He repeated many of his ideas in 1910 in an article based on lectures given before the graduating engineering class of Columbia University. In it he included a complicated diagram whose most interesting feature is the recognition that the fixed costs will jump as a company increases the number of machines employed.[1]

SIR JOHN MANN

It was not only in the United States that the ideas of break-even analysis were becoming known at the beginning of the twentieth century. Writing on 'Oncost or Expenses' in the *Encyclopaedia of Accounting*[2] (published in Edinburgh in 1904), the Scottish chartered accountant Sir John Mann showed himself fully aware of the implications of fixed charges: 'it may be expedient to sell at a price which yields enough to pay for wages and material with something left over in addition, however small, towards oncost – let the contribution towards oncost be ever so little, it is better than no contribution at all'. He set out the diagram shown in Fig. 4.3 (although he did not give it a name) and commented:

This [diagram] shows the foundation line of the 'bedrock' fixed charges remaining steady throughout; added thereon is the rising amount of the varying charges, by a line indicating the total of the fixed and varying charges. By introducing a line for the total earnings of the machines, calculated at the assumed normal rates, the diagram shows that when on half-time the normal earnings of the machines are not sufficient to meet even the fixed charges; but as the volume of work grows, the deficit between the earnings and the total charges diminishes until the normal point is reached. Thereafter a surplus emerges, and to

[1] Henry Hess, 'Manufacturing Profits and Losses', in *Engineering Magazine*, XXXIX (1910) 892–8.
[2] Sir John Mann, 'Oncost or Expenses', in *Encyclopaedia of Accounting*, ed. G. Lisle, 8 vols (Edinburgh, William Green & Sons, 1903–7) v 199–225.

indicate the theoretical expansion of this surplus the lines are continued to a point where the works are assumed to run day and night without intermission. ...

Where a manufacturer or engineer is prepared to devote a little time and thought to the study of his oncost problems, he will find that valuable results will readily be reached by the separation of the fixed and the fluctuating elements of expense. By the use of diagrams which can easily be constructed for him by his subordinates from existing data, and continued from month to month, he can obtain an accurate and helpful grasp of the trend of his affairs and their varying relations. For instance, [in the diagram reproduced], if we substitute for the line indicating the earnings of the machines, the total turnover or revenue of the business, the shaded portion (being the deficit or surplus of machine earnings compared with the total charges) serves to indicate the net loss or profit of the business.[1]

It is interesting to note that Mann did not start his graph at the point of zero production.

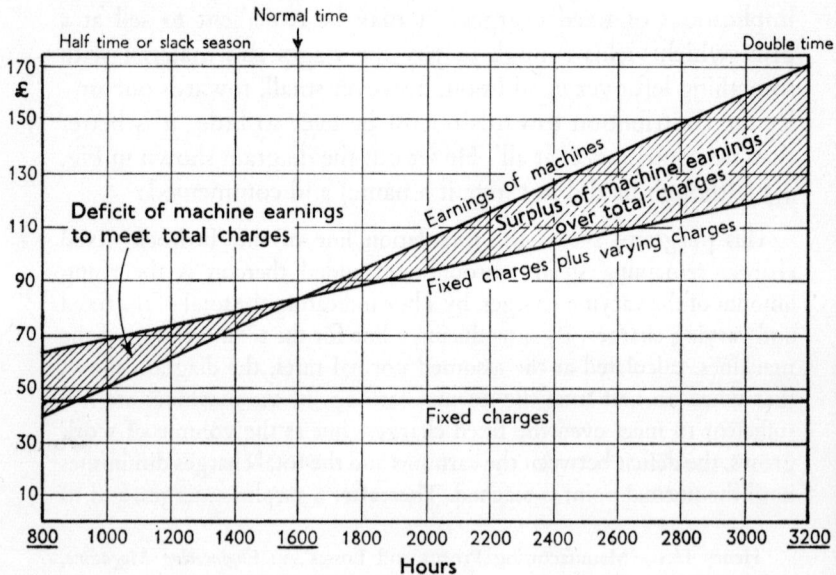

Fig. 4.3 Sir John Mann's diagram (1904)

[1] Ibid. pp. 217-18.

KNOEPPEL, RAUTENSTRAUCH AND WILLIAMS

During the 1920's and 1930's break-even analysis was further developed by a number of American industrial engineers – notably C. E. Knoeppel, Walter Rautenstrauch and John H. Williams.[1] Knoeppel described himself as 'a believer in the doctrines of Frederick W. Taylor and Henry L. Gantt' and 'a disciple and associate of Harrington Emerson'[2] (one of the pioneers of standard costing). According to his own account, Knoeppel's first introduction to the subject was through reading Hess's articles on wage-payment methods published in the *Engineering Magazine* in 1904.[3] Curiously enough he seems never to have read Hess's more relevant article of 1903.

In 1909 Knoeppel devised for the Struthers-Wells Company of Warren, Pennsylvania, what he described as a 'rather crude crossover chart'.[4] This he later published in his book *Graphic Production Control* (1920) (see Fig. 4.4 below), with the comment that it illustrated the manner of showing graphically a business as a whole, so as to be able to tell where losses end and profits begin.[5]

Perhaps Knoeppel's most important contribution was to clearly link his graphical analysis to the technique of flexible budgeting. He described his chart (which he called a 'profitgraph') as 'essentially a *graphic master budget*, for a year or shorter period' and '*a graphic variable budgeted income statement*'. He warned that the profitgraph was 'merely the plan on chart paper of scientific budgeting – *variable budgeting* – and if this is well done the Profitgraph will take care of itself'.[6] It is in some ways a pity that

---

[1] There are biographies of Knoeppel and Williams in *The Golden Book of Management*, ed. L. Urwick (London, Newman Neame, 1956).

[2] C. E. Knoeppel, *Profit Engineering* (New York, McGraw-Hill, 1933) p. ix.

[3] H. Hess, 'Wage-Paying Methods from the Viewpoint of the Workman', in *Engineering Magazine*, XXVII (1904) 27–35; 'Wage-Paying Methods from the Viewpoint of the Employer', ibid. pp. 172–86; 'Wage-Paying Methods from the Viewpoint of the Invested Capital', ibid. pp. 409–16.

[4] Knoeppel, *Profit Engineering*, pp. 82–5, for his account of the 'genesis of the profitgraph'.

[5] C. E. Knoeppel, *Graphic Production Control* (New York, Engineering Magazine Co., 1920) pp. 376, 378.

[6] *Profit Engineering*, pp. 91, 111, 310.

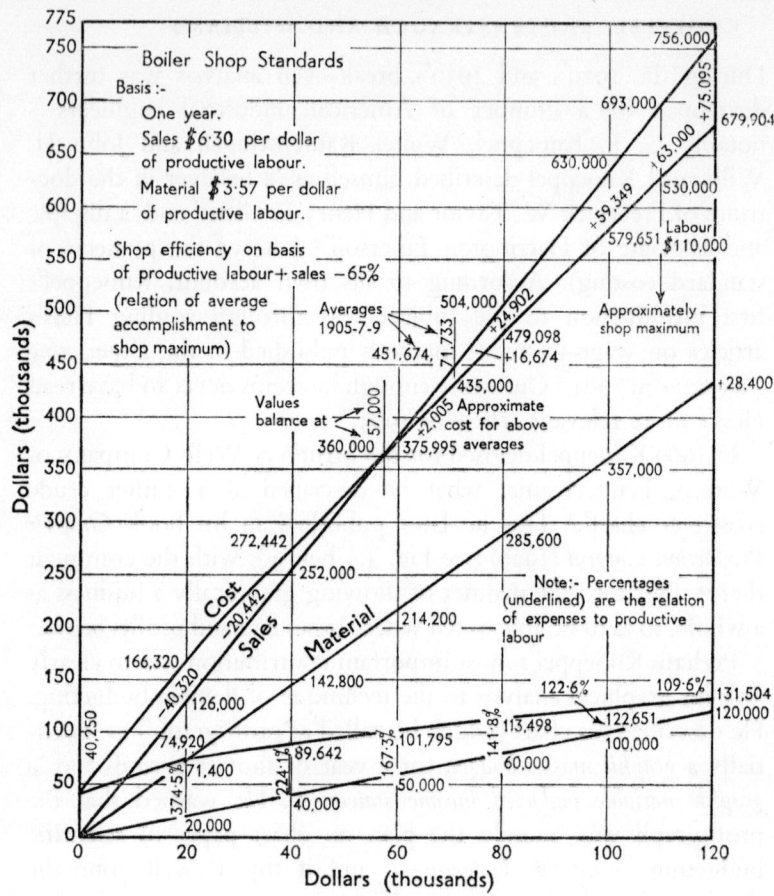

Fig. 4.4 Shop Standards at Different Capacities (C. E. Knoeppel, 1920)

his term profitgraph did not stick since the chart is more useful as a graphical budget than as an indicator of the break-even point of a business.

Knoeppel believed that most total-cost curves were linear within the range 25–90 per cent of capacity and argued that 'grouped straight-line trends give an over-all result that is approximately correct, with much less effort and in much shorter time, and materially simplify the arithmetical calculations'.[1]

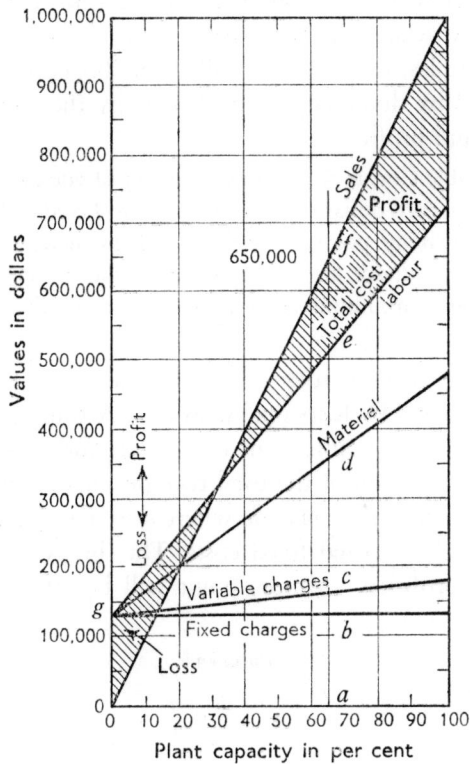

Fig. 4.5 The Graphic Basis of a Budget (W. Rautenstrauch, 1922)

None of the economists, engineers and accountants mentioned so far used the term 'break-even chart'. This phrase was first used by Walter Rautenstrauch who appears to have developed his ideas independently of Hess, Mann and Knoeppel.[2] Rautenstrauch first

[1] *Managing for Profit*, pp. 122–3.
[2] See R. Villers, 'The Origin of the Break-Even Chart', in *Journal of Business* XXVIII (1955) 296–7, commenting on N. Chapin, 'The Development of the Break-Even Chart', in *Journal of Business*, XXVIII (1955) 148–9.

published his chart (Fig. 4.5 above) in 1922[1] He described his chart as the 'graphic basis of a budget' and pointed out that the intersection of the sales line with the total-cost line 'will indicate the volume at which the company will "break-even"'.

In the same year John H. Williams showed, by means of arithmetical examples, that what he called the 'breaking point' could be calculated by dividing the fixed costs by the contribution to fixed costs and profit:

> If the Variable Cost is $0.80 of every dollar of sales, obviously there is only $0.20 of each dollar of sales applicable to Fixed Cost. Therefore, to find the breaking point, or point at which there will be neither profit or loss, we divide $0.20 into $120,000 [the amount of the Fixed Cost] which gives us the answer of $600,000 per month as the breaking point.[2]

The simple mathematics of break-even were published by Rautenstrauch and by Knoeppel's associate Arthur J. Minor in the early 1930's.[3] Both pointed out that, given their assumptions of linearity, the equation of the total revenue curve is $y = x$ and of the total cost curve $y' = mx + b$, where $m =$ the slope of the total cost curve and $b =$ total fixed costs. The 'break-even' (Rautenstrauch) or 'profitless' (Minor) point will be where $y = y'$, i.e. where

$$x = mx + b$$
$$= \frac{b}{(1 - m)}.$$

This is called by Rautenstrauch the law of vanishing profits and by Minor the fundamental equation. Translating the algebra into

---

[1] W. Rautenstrauch, 'The Budget as a Means of Industrial Control', in *Chemical and Metallurgical Engineering*, XXVII (1922) 415-16. No attempt is made here to list the many later books and articles in which Rautenstrauch makes use of break-even charts.

[2] John H. Williams, 'A Technique for the Chief Executive', in *Bulletin of the Taylor Society*, VII (1922) 51. This article did not include any charts. A chart from his book *The Flexible Budget* (New York, McGraw-Hill, 1934) is reproduced in C. Weber, *The Evolution of Direct Costing* (Urbana, Ill., Center for International Education and Research in Accounting, 1966) p. 31.

[3] W. Rautenstrauch, *The Successful Control of Profits* (New York, B. C. Forbes,

THE ORIGINS OF THE BREAK-EVEN CHART 71

words and using Rautenstrauch's terminology the break-even point occurs at the volume equal to

$$1 - \frac{\text{Constant Total Costs}}{\dfrac{\text{Variable Total Costs}}{\text{Corresponding Sales}}}$$

Both writers then go on to develop a number of other useful equations.

DEVELOPMENTS SINCE THE 1930'S

This chapter has been concerned with origins and it is not proposed to trace in detail the later history of the break-even chart. During the 1930's its use spread from engineers to accountants; profit-volume charts showing the relationship between net profit and volume were also used.[1] Break-even analysis has not, however, appealed very much to economists who have tended to regard its linear cost and revenue functions with disdain. Machlup, for example, regards break-even charts as 'nothing but glamorised multiplication tables, doing a bit of simple arithmetic which a person of average intelligence could have learned to do in his head'.[2] Wiles refers to 'the so-called break-even diagram, taught in schools of business' and describes the assumptions on which it is based as false.[3] In reply it can be argued that *over the relevant ranges of production* the total cost curve often is linear: 'the various short-run studies more often than not indicate constant marginal cost and declining average cost as the pattern that best seems to describe the data that have been analyzed'.[4]

1930) pp. 108–9, 135–6, and 'The Economic Characteristics of the Manufacturing Industries', in *Mechanical Engineering*, LIV (1932) 763–5; Arthur J. Minor, 'Mathematics behind the Profitgraph', in *Profit Engineering*, ch. xv.

[1] See, for example, S. A. Peck, 'The Managerial Aspect of Controls', in *N.A.C.A. Bulletin*, 15 Dec. 1938.

[2] F. Machlup, *The Economics of Sellers' Competition* (Baltimore, Johns Hopkins Press, 1952) p. 77.

[3] P. J. D. Wiles, *Price, Cost and Output* (Oxford, Basil Blackwell, 1956) pp. 50–1.

[4] J. Johnston, *Statistical Cost Analysis* (New York, McGraw-Hill, 1960) p. 168. See also the discussion in A. D. Barton, 'The Break-Even Chart', in *Australian Accountant*, XXVI (1956).

More recently a number of writers have shown how break-even analysis can be improved by linking it with linear programming.[1]

SUMMARY

The break-even chart is a simple mathematical model based upon the distinction between fixed and variable costs. This distinction first became of practical importance during the Industrial Revolution and was recognised by a number of nineteenth-century economists. The break-even chart was developed independently by the American engineers, Hess, Knoeppel, Rautenstrauch and Williams and their associates, and by the Scottish accountant Sir John Mann.

[1] R. K. Jaedicke, 'Improving Break-Even Analysis by Linear Programming', in *N.A.A. Bulletin* Sec. 1, Mar. 1961; A. Charnes, W. W. Cooper and Y. Ijiri, 'Breakeven Budgeting and Programming to Goals', in *Journal of Accounting Research*, 1 (1963) reprinted in H. R. Anton and P. A. Firmin, *Contemporary Issues in Cost Accounting* (Boston, Houghton Mifflin, 1966).

The five diagrams reproduced in this chapter are redrawings of the originals. In the interests of clarity, a number of minor changes in typography have been made.

PART TWO

HISTORICAL PERSPECTIVE

5 Select Bibliography of Works on the History of Accounting[1]

THE difficulty of compiling a select bibliography lies not so much in deciding what to include as in deciding what to leave out. I have excluded works which in my opinion add little or nothing to our understanding and knowledge of accounting history or which have been superseded by later writings. Some articles have been excluded because they have later appeared (not necessarily in the same guise) as parts of books. In some cases the bibliography is merely representative: no attempt, for example, has been made to include all the British manorial and parochial accounts which have been reprinted, or to include all the histories of accounting firms which have been published.

Entries followed by § are printed in *Studies in the History of Accounting*, A. C. Littleton and B. S. Yamey (eds.) (London, Sweet & Maxwell, and Homewood, Ill., Irwin, 1956). Some works are included which I have not had the opportunity of examining. These are marked †. I am sure that I have missed some worthy items, especially those which have been published in languages other than English. I shall be glad to hear of items which may at some time be included in a supplementary list.

The arrangement of the bibliography is as follows:

    A. General
    B. Ancient Accounting
    C. Early Italian Accounting
    D. Early Netherlands Accounting
    E. Early French Accounting
    F. Early English and Scottish Accounting
        (i) Manorial, Household and Parochial Accounts
        (ii) Mercantile Accounts
        (iii) Government Accounts
    G. Early Irish Accounting

[1] First published in *Abacus*, 1 (1965) 62–84. Extensive revisions have been made for this reprinting. The author is grateful for the help of R. P. Brooker, R. G. Dryen, L. Goldberg, H. P. Hain and B. S. Yamey, but is solely responsible for any imperfections which remain.

76 MANAGEMENT ACCOUNTING

    H. Early German and Austrian Accounting
    I. Early American Accounting
    J. Early Australian Accounting
    K. Early Japanese Accounting
    L. Early Indian Accounting
    M. Professional Accountancy
    N. Auditing
    O. Cost and Management Accounting
    P. Corporate Accounting
    Q. Mechanised Accounting and Computers
    R. Executorship Accounting
    S. Financial Accounting Theory
    T. Education
    U. Terminology
    V. Bibliographies, Biographies and Chronologies
    W. Bank Accounting
    X. Miscellaneous
       Index of Authors

A. GENERAL

1. BESTA, F., *La Ragioneria*, 3 vols (Milan, F. Vallardi, 2nd ed., 1922). This work contains several historical chapters; see Littleton and Yamey (described below) p. 114, n. 1.
2. BROWN, R. (ed.), *History of Accounting and Accountants* (Edinburgh, Jack, 1905; reprinted by B. Franklin, New York, 1966) 459 pp. The most important of the early British works. Still very useful although obviously dated in many respects. Contains a chronological list of printed books on book-keeping, 1494-1800.
3. BURSK, E. C., CLARK, D. T., and HIDY, R. W., *The World of Business* (New York, Simon & Schuster, 1962) vol. I, pt. II, pp. 61-154. Contains among other things a reprint of the first sixteen chapters of Geijsbeek's translation of the book-keeping section of Pacioli's *Summa* (see below).
4. DE ROOVER, R., 'Aux origines d'une technique intellectuelle: la formation et l'expansion de la comptabilité à partie double', *Annales d'histoire économique et sociale*, IX (1937) 171-93, 270-98. Not entirely superseded by de Roover's later writings.

SELECT BIBLIOGRAPHY 77

5. ELDRIDGE, H. J., *Evolution of the Science of Book-keeping* (London, Gee, 1931; Revised 2nd ed. by FRANKLAND, L., 1954) 70 pp.
    A useful short account, consisting mainly of descriptions of books.
6. FOSTER, B. F., *The Origin and Progress of Book-keeping* (London, C. H. Law, 1852) 54 pp.
    An account of works (mainly British and American) on book-keeping published 1494–1851.
7. GEIJSBEEK, J. B., *Ancient Double-Entry Book-keeping* (Denver, Colorado, J. B. Geijsbeek, 1914) 182 pp.
    Contains a reproduction and translation of the book-keeping section of Pacioli's *Summa* and also abstracts from the works of Manzoni, Pietra, Mainardi, Ympyn, Stevin and Dafforne. Out of print. Part of the translation of Pacioli has been reprinted in Bursk, Clark and Hidy (see above).
8. GOMBERG, L., *Histoire critique de la Théorie des Comptes* (Geneva, L. Gomberg, and Berlin, L. Weiss, 1929) 82 pp.
    History of European theories of double entry.
9. GONZALEZ FERRANDO, J. M., *Historia y Doctrinas de la Contabilidad por Joseph-H. Vlaemminck . . . Version española, revisada y ampliada* (Madrid, Editorial E.J.E.S., 1961) 429 pp.†
    A Spanish translation of item 30, amplified mainly in respect of Spain; has a long bibliography not in 30.
10. GREEN, W. L., *History and Survey of Accountancy* (Brooklyn, Standard Text Press, 1930) 288 pp.
    Includes chapters on the history of book-keeping, legislation and education for the accountancy profession and societies of accountants.
11. HATFIELD, H. R., 'An Historical Defense of Book-keeping', *Journal of Accountancy*, XXXVII (1924) 241–53; reprinted in BAXTER, W. T., and DAVIDSON, S. (eds), *Studies in Accounting Theory* (London, Sweet & Maxwell, 2nd ed., 1962) pp. 1–13; MOONITZ, M., and LITTLETON, A. C., *Significant Accounting Essays* (Englewood Cliffs, N.J., Prentice-Hall, 1965) pp. 3–13; and in *Journal of Industrial Engineering*, XVII (1966) 287–92.
    A witty article written 'to remove the stigma attached to accounting by showing that in its origin it is respectable, nay, even academic'.

78 MANAGEMENT ACCOUNTING

12. HAULOTTE, R., *Théorie spéculative de la comptabilité appuyée par l'Histoire* (Brussels, Éditions Comptabilité et Productivité, n.d.) 128 pp.

   A study of book-keeping up to the appearance of double entry.

13. JÄGER, E. L., *Beiträge zur Geschichte der Doppelbuchhaltung* (Stuttgart, Kröner, 1874) xiv+289 pp.

   Deals with the works of Manzoni, Pietra, Savary, de la Porte and others.

14. JÄGER, E. L., *Lucas Paccioli und Simon Stevin* (Stuttgart, Kröner, 1876) xvi+216 pp.

15. KATS, P., 'Early History of Book-keeping by Double Entry', *Journal of Accountancy*, XLVII (1929) 203–10, 275–90.

   A general survey, stressing factors' accounts.

16. KHEIL, C. P., *Ueber einige ältere Bearbeitungen des Buchhaltungs-Tractates von Luca Pacioli* (Prague, Bursik & Kohout, 1896) 128 pp.

17. KOJIMA, O., *Studies in the History of Book-keeping* (Tokyo, Moriyama-Shoten Ltd, 1964).

   In Japanese with an English summary. Contains interesting material on several accounting historians.

18. LITTLETON, A. C., *Accounting Evolution to 1900* (New York, American Institute Publishing Co., 1933; reprinted by Russell & Russell, New York, 1967) 373 pp.

   Although written over thirty years ago, this is still the most important book in English on accounting history by one author.

19. LITTLETON, A. C., *Essays on Accountancy* (Urbana, University of Illinois Press, 1961) Part One. 'On Accounting History', pp. 1–188.

   Selections from Littleton's historical writings drawn from *Accounting Evolution to 1900* (see above), *Accounting Review*, *Journal of Accountancy*, *Structure of Accounting Theory* (Menasha, Wis., American Accounting Association, 1953), *New York Certified Public Accountant* and other sources.

20. LITTLETON, A. C., and YAMEY, B. S. (eds), *Studies in the History of Accounting* (London, Sweet & Maxwell, and Homewood, Ill., Irwin, 1956) 392 pp.

   The most comprehensive modern work in English. The matters treated by the twenty-four contributors range in time from the fifth century B.C. to A.D. 1900 and in space from England to Australia. Many of the contributions are cited individually in this bibliography.

SELECT BIBLIOGRAPHY 79

21. LITTLETON, A. C., and ZIMMERMAN, V. K., *Accounting Theory: Continuity and Change* (Englewood Cliffs, N.J., Prentice-Hall, 1962) 292 pp.

    A history of accounting thought rather than accounting practice. Its theme is that 'Continuity in the midst of change has typified the development of accounting' (p. 256). Good bibliography.

22. LOPEZ, R. S., and RAYMOND, I. W., *Medieval Trade in the Mediterranean World* (New York, Columbia University Press, 1955) ch. 22, 'The Progress of Accounting Methods', pp. 359-77.

    Includes extracts from Provençal and Italian account books of the fourteenth century and from Benedetto Cotrugli's *Della mercature et del mercante perfetto* (Naples, 1458).

23. MELIS, F., *Storia della Ragioneria* (Bologna, Dott. Cesare Zuffi, 1950) 872 pp.

    The standard Italian work. Traces the history of accounting from the ancient world to the twentieth century A.D. with an emphasis on Italian developments. Extensive bibliography but no index. Has not been translated into English.

24. MURRAY, D., *Chapters in the History of Book-keeping, Accountancy, and Commercial Arithmetic* (Glasgow, Jackson, Wylie, 1930) 519 pp.

    Sections on: book-keeping and accountancy in Scotland in the seventeenth and eighteenth centuries; book-keeping and accountancy in early times; judicial accounting; some writers on book-keeping; early arithmetic; some writers on commercial arithmetic and book-keeping.

25. PELOUBET, M. E., 'The Historical Development of Accounting', pp. 5-27 of BACKER, M. (ed.), *Modern Accounting Theory* (Englewood Cliffs, N.J., Prentice-Hall, 1966).

    A short survey mainly concerned with British and American developments in the nineteenth and twentieth centuries.

26. PERAGALLO, E., *Origin and Evolution of Double Entry Book-keeping, A Study of Italian Practice from the Fourteenth Century* (New York, American Institute Publishing Co., 1938) 157 pp.

    A beautifully produced book mainly concerned with Italian and French accounting practice and theory. Contains one of the few discussions in English of the *cinquecontisti* school and of logismography.

27. PERAGALLO, E., 'Origin of the Trial Balance', § pp. 215-22.

    Neither Pacioli's *bilancio del libro* nor his *summa summarum* was trial balances, but Pacioli did know the function of a trial balance. See also Peragallo's two articles of the same name in *Journal of Accountancy*, LXXII (1941) 448–54, and *Accounting Review*, XXXI (1956) 389–94.

28. SOLOMONS, D., 'The Maner and Fourme how to keepe a Perfecte Reconyng', *Lloyds Bank Review*, XLIII (1957) 34–46.

    A review article of Littleton and Yamey's *Studies in the History of Accounting* (see above).

29. [THOMSON, H. W.], *The Earliest Books on Book-keeping 1494 to 1683* (London, Institute of Chartered Accountants in England and Wales, 1963) 16 pp.

    Brief accounts of the first books on double entry in Italian, Flemish, French, German and Spanish and their authors.

30. VLAEMMINCK, J.-H., *Histoire et Doctrines de la Comptabilité* (Brussels, Éditions du Truerenberg, 1956) 231 pp.

    A relatively short survey written in Belgium. Begins with Sumerian accounting and ends with modern management accounting. Very little on accounting developments in English-speaking countries. Has not been translated into English.

31. WOOLF, A. H., *A Short History of Accountants and Accountancy* (London, Gee, 1912) 254 pp.

    After Brown the best of the early British works. Contains a bibliography compiled by Cosmo Gordon of books on accounting 1494–1800.

32. YAMEY, B. S., 'Scientific Book-keeping and the Rise of Capitalism', *Economic History Review*, 2nd ser., I (1949) 99–113; reprinted in BAXTER, W. T. (ed.), *Studies in Accounting* (London, Sweet & Maxwell, 1950) pp. 13–30.

    A criticism of Sombart's thesis that the double-entry system played an important part in releasing, activating, stimulating or accentuating the 'rationalistic pursuit of unlimited profits', an essential element in the capitalistic spirit.

33. YAMEY, B. S., 'Accounting and the Rise of Capitalism: Further Notes on a Theme by Sombart', *Studi in Onore di Amintore Fanfani* (Milan, Dott. A. Giuffre, 1962) vol. 6, pp. 833–57, and *Journal of Accounting Research*, II (1964) 117–36.

    The author maintains the position taken up by him in his 1949 article.

34. YAMEY, B. S., 'The Functional Development of Double-Entry Bookkeeping', *Accountant*, CIII (1940) 333–42.

   A general discussion, including reference to the association of double entry with debtor–creditor relationships.

35. YAMEY, B. S., 'Notes on the Origin of Double-Entry Bookkeeping', *Accounting Review*, XXII (1947) 263–72.

   A discussion of the possible influence of agency book-keeping on the origins of double entry.

36. YAMEY, B. S., 'Fifteenth and Sixteenth Century Manuscripts on the Art of Book-keeping', *Journal of Accounting Research*, V (1967) 51–76.

   Includes, *inter alia*, discussions of Matthäus Schwarz's manuscript (see Weitnauer, item 184 below) and Pacioli's supposed manuscript source.

B. ANCIENT ACCOUNTING

37. CHIERA, E., *Selected Temple Accounts from Telloch, Yokha and Drehem* (Philadelphia, University of Pennsylvania, 1921) 40 pp.+ 36 plates.

   Reproductions and partial translations of clay tablets from southern Babylonia (twenty-third and twenty-fourth centuries, B.C.).

38. DELMOUZOU-PEPPA, D., *The Institution of Public Accountants in Ancient Greece* (Athens, Institute of Certified Public Accountants of Greece, 1963) 17 pp.+v plates.

   The evidence for public accounting in classical Greece.

39. GRIER, E., *Accounting in the Zenon Papyri* (New York, Columbia University Press, 1934) 77 pp.

   A study of accounting methods in Ptolemaic Egypt in the third century B.C.

40. HAIN, H. P., 'Accounting Control in the Zenon Papyri', *Accounting Review*, XLI (1966) 699–703.

   A commentary on Ptolemaic accounting.

41. JONES, T. B., 'Book-keeping in Ancient Sumer', *Archaeology*, IX (1956) 16–21.
    Record-keeping on clay tablets.
42. KEISTER, O. R., 'Commercial Record-Keeping in Ancient Mesopotamia', *Accounting Review*, XXXVIII (1963) 371–6.
    In the words of the author, 'a much abbreviated summary of the types of records kept by the ancient Mesopotamian people [with] appropriate tablet translations'.
43. KEISTER, O. R., 'The Mechanics of Mesopotamian Record-Keeping', *N.A.A. Bulletin*, XLVI (1965) 18–24.
    Cuneiform writing and numbering in ancient Mesopotamia.
44. MERRITT, B. D., *Athenian Financial Documents of the Fifth Century* (Ann Arbor, University of Michigan Press, 1932) 192 pp.
    Contains transcriptions, translations and comment on Athenian public accounts of the fifth century B.C.
45. MICKWITZ, G., 'Economic Rationalism in Graeco-Roman Agriculture', *English Historical Review*, LII (1937) 577–89.
    Analyses the aims and achievements of the accounting systems of Graeco-Roman landowners.
46. STE. CROIX, G. E. M. DE, 'Greek and Roman Accounting'. § pp. 14–74.
    An important article. Ste. Croix concludes that Greek and Roman book-keeping, 'minutely detailed as it often was, remained rudimentary in method and never grew into an integrated double-entry complex, with interlocking accounts, or even into a unified single entry system', but 'took the form of individual records of debts and of receipts and payments, and miscellaneous inventories, rather than accounts in the modern sense' (pp. 14–15).

C. EARLY ITALIAN ACCOUNTING

47. BOURSY, A. V., 'The Name of Paciolo', *Accounting Review*, XVIII (1943) 205–9.
    Boursy claims that the only correct spellings are the Latin Paciolus and the Italian variants Paciuolo and Paciolo.

48. BROWN, R. G., and JOHNSTON, K. S., *Paciolo on Accounting* (New York, McGraw-Hill, 1963) 144 pp.
    The most recent English translation of the book-keeping section of Pacioli's *Summa*. Also contains a short biography and a reproduction of the original Italian text. See review by Yamey, *Accountancy*, LXXVI (1965) 244–5.
49. CASTELLANI, A., *Nuovi testi fiorentini del Dugento* (Florence, G. C. Sansoni, 1952) 1 vol. in 2 pts, xii+946 pp.
    Reprints of thirteenth-century Florentine texts, mainly fragments of account books. See de Roover in *Accounting Review*, XXX (1955) 406–7.
50. CHIAUDANO, M. (ed.), *Libro Vermiglio di Corte di Roma e di Avignone del Segnale del C, della Compagnia Fiorentina di Iacopo Girolami, Filippo Corbizzi e Tommaso Corbizzi, 1332–1337* (Turin, V. Bona Tipografio, 1963) 212 pp. †
    Reproduces the ledger of a small fourteenth-century Florentine firm.
51. CRIVELLI, P., *An Original Translation of the Treatise on Double Entry Book-keeping by Frater Lucas Pacioli* (London, Institute of Book-keepers, 1924) 120 pp.
    One of the three English translations of the book-keeping section of Pacioli's *Summa*.
52. DE ROOVER, Florence Edler, *Glossary of Medieval Terms of Business. Italian Series 1200–1600* (Cambridge, Mass., Medieval Academy of America, 1934) xx+430 pp.
    Contains much information on medieval Italian accounting procedures.
53. DE ROOVER, Florence Edler, 'Partnership Accounts in Twelfth Century Genoa', *Bulletin of the Business Historical Society*, XV (1941) 87–92.§
    The accounts discussed relate to the winding up of three Genoese partnerships during the years 1156–8. They are the oldest known medieval business-records.
54. DE ROOVER, R., 'The Development of Accounting prior to Luca Pacioli according to the Account-Books of Medieval Merchants',§ pp. 114–84.
    An important survey of European (mainly Italian) accounting developments during the three and a half centuries before the publication of Pacioli's treatise in 1494. This article in effect

constitutes a bibliography of books and articles on actual account books before 1494.
55. DE ROOVER, R., 'Paciolo or Pacioli?', *Accounting Review*, XIX (1944) 68–9.
A comment on Boursy's article (see above).
56. GITTI, V. (ed.), *Trattato de' computi e delle scriture* (Turin, Camilla e Bertolero, 3rd ed., 1878) 142 pp.
An edited Italian text of the book-keeping section of Pacioli's *Summa*.
57. HAULOTTE, R., and STEVELINCK, E., *Luca Pacioli: sa vie, son œuvre et la première traduction en français du premier traité de comptabilité imprimé en 1494 à Venise* (Brussels, Éditions Comptabilité et Productivité, 1962) 94 pp.
A short biography of Pacioli followed by the first French translation of Tractatus XI of the *Summa*.
58. HEERS, J., *Le Livre de Comptes de Giovanni Piccamiglio, homme d'affaires Génois 1456–1459* (Paris, S.E.V.P.E.N., 1959) 377 pp.
The accounts (in double entry) of a mid-fifteenth-century Genoese businessman.
59. KATS, P., 'Benedetto Cotrugli van Ragusa', *Maandblad voor het Boekhouden*, XXXII (1925–6) 32–5.†
Translation into Dutch and commentary on Cotrugli's section on book-keeping.
60. KHEIL, C. P., *Benedetto Cotrugli Raugeo* (Vienna, 1906) 36 pp.
Reproduces the Italian text of Cotrugli's section on book-keeping together with a German translation.
61. LANE, F. C., 'Venture Accounting in Medieval Business Management', *Bulletin of the Business Historical Society*, XIX (1945) 164–73.
Mercantile operations were divided into ventures and in computing profit or loss each venture was treated as an independent unit.
62. LANE, F. C., *Andrea Barbarigo, Merchant of Venice, 1418–1449* (Baltimore, Johns Hopkins University Studies in Historical and Political Science, LXII i (1944) 224 pp.
Critical Note II, pp. 153–81, discusses accounting methods in some detail and there are many other references to accounting.
63. MELIS, F., 'La Contabilità', pt. IV, pp. 339–452 of *Aspetti della Vita Economica Medievale (studi nell'archivio Datini di Prato)* (Siena, Monte dei Paschi di Siena, vol. I, 1962).

64. PENNDORF, B., *Luca Pacioli. Abhandlung über die Buchhaltung, 1494* (Stuttgart, C. E. Poeschel, 1933) x+162 pp.
A German translation of Pacioli's treatise. Lengthy introduction.
65. SAPORI, A., *I libri degli Alberti del Guidice* (Milan, Garzanti, 1952) xcii+365 pp.
Fragments of the account books of the Alberti family of merchant bankers. Includes a list of published medieval Italian account books. See also DE ROOVER, *Accounting Review*, XXX (1955) 407-8, and his 'The Story of the Alberti Company of Florence, 1302-1348, as Revealed in its Account Books', *Business History Review*, XXXII (1958) 14-59.
66. TAYLOR, R. E., *No Royal Road: Luca Pacioli and his Times* (Chapel Hill, University of North Carolina Press, 1942) ix+445 pp.
The standard biography in English. See also Taylor's article in Littleton and Yamey.
67. TAYLOR, R. E., 'The Name of Pacioli', *Accounting Review*, XIX (1944) 69-76.
A reply to Boursy's article (see above). Taylor's choice is *Pacioli*: 'but any other spelling that anyone cares to use will be all right with me'.
68. ZERBI, T., *Le Origini della Partita Doppia* (Milan, Marzorati, 1952) 521 pp.
An important study of the origins of double-entry bookkeeping in Italy. Good bibliography. Contains five page summaries in Italian, French, English and German. There is no English translation of the whole work.

D. EARLY NETHERLANDS ACCOUNTING

69. BRULEZ, W., *De Firma Della Faille en de Internationale Handel van Vlaamse Firma's in de 16e Eeuw* (Brussels, Paleis der Academiën, 1959) 634 pp.
Chapter 14 (pp. 432-44) describes and discusses the bookkeeping methods of this sixteenth-century firm of merchants.

70. CARMAN, L. A., 'Researches of Raymond de Roover in Flemish Accounting of the fourteenth century', *Journal of Accountancy*, LX (1935) 111-22.
   English summary of de Roover's book on Ruyelle (item 74 below).
71. CRONE, E., DIJKSTERHUIS, E. J., FORBES, R. J., MINNAERT, M. G. J., and PANNEKOEK, A. (eds), *The Principal Works of Simon Stevin*, 5 vols (Amsterdam, C. V. Swets & Zeitlinger, 1955-66).
   The General Introduction (vol. I, pp. 1-34) and the reproduction with translation and introduction of *Tables of Interest* (1582) (vol. 2A, pp. 13-117) are of some interest to historians of accounting. Stevin's work on book-keeping is not included.
72. DENUCÉ, J., *Inventaire des Affaitadi, banquiers italiens à Anvers, de l'Année 1568* (Antwerp, Éditions de 'Sikkel', 1934) 263 pp.
   Includes the text of the inventory (in Italian). See also GORIS, J. A., *Étude sur les colonies marchandes méridionales (portugais, espagnols, italiens), à Anvers de 1488 à 1567* (Louvain, Librairie Universitaire, 1925) pp. 121-7, 629-30.
73. DE ROOVER, R., *Jan Ympyn* (Antwerp, Veritas, 1928) 30 pp.
   A short study of the first Flemish book on double-entry book-keeping.
74. DE ROOVER, R., *Le Livre de comptes de Guillaume Ruyelle, changeur à Bruges (1369)* (Bruges, reprinted from *Annales de la Société d'Émulation de Bruges*, vol. 57, 1934) 95 pp.
   The accounts of a fourteenth-century money-changer.
75. DE ROOVER, R., 'Something New About Jan Ympyn Christoffels', *Accountant*, XCVII (1937) 657-8.
   A summary of 'Een en ander over Jan Ympyn Christoffels', *Tijdschrift voor Geschiedenis*, LII (1937) 163-79.†
76. DE WAAL, P. G. A., *De Leer van het boekhouden in de Nederlanden tijdens de zestiende eeuw* (Roermond, J. J. Romen & Zonen, 1927) 318 pp.
   Book-keeping in the Netherlands in the sixteenth century.
77. DE WAAL, P. G. A., 'De Engelsche vertaling van Jan Impyn's Nieuwe Instructie', *Economisch-Historisch Jaarboek*, XVIII (1934) 1-58.†
   The English translation of Ympyn's book.
78. DUVERGER, E., *Jan, Jacques en Frans De Moor, Tapijtwevers en Tapijthandelaars te Oudenaarde, Antwerpen en Gent (1560 tot ca.*

1680) (Ghent, Centre Universitaire d'étude de l'histoire de la tapisserie flamande, 1960).†
Reproduces a ledger of Frans.

79. KUPERUS, J. A., 'Boekhoudingen op Nederlanse Landbouwbedrijven vóór 1900', pp. 79–111 of *Ceres en Clio* (Wageningen, H. Veenman & Zonen N.V., 1964).
Farms accounting in the Netherlands before 1900. There is a one-page summary in English.

80. TEN HAVE, O., *De Leer van het Boekhouden in de Nederlanden tijdens de zeventiende en achttiende Eeuw* (Delft, N.V. Technische Boekhandel en Drukkerij J. Waltman Jr, 1934) 305 pp.
Book-keeping in the Netherlands in the seventeenth and eighteenth centuries.

81. TEN HAVE, O., 'Simon Stevin of Bruges',§ pp. 236–46.
A short account of Stevin's life (1548–1620) and work.

82. KHEIL, C. P., *Valentin Mennher und Antioch Rocha 1550–1565* (Prague, Bursik & Kohout, 1898) 59 pp.
Mennher's book and Rocha's Spanish translation of it.

83. SARTON, G., 'Simon Stevin of Bruges (1548–1620)', *Isis* XXI (1934) 241–303; reprinted in D. STIMSON (ed.), *Sarton on the History of Science* (Cambridge, Mass., Harvard University Press, 1962) pp. 149–88.
Biographical and bibliographical. Includes a description of Stevin's *Livre de compte de prince à la manière d'Italie . . .* (Leiden, 1608).

84. SLICHER VAN BATH, B. H., 'Een Fries Landbouwbedrijf in de tweede helft van de Zestiende eeuw', *Agronomisch-Historische Bijdragen* IV (1958) 69–208.†
Friesian agricultural accounts in the second half of the sixteenth century.

85. VOLMER, J. G. Ch., *Mennher de Kempten. Practique brifue pour tenir liures de compte à la guise et manière Italiana. Publié d'après l'édition de 1550 par J. G. Ch. Volmer* (Utrecht, J. Van Druten, 1894) xix pp.+ unpaged reproduction.
A reproduction of Mennher's book.

E. EARLY FRENCH ACCOUNTING

86. BLANC, A., *Le Livre de comptes de Jacme Olivier, marchand narbonnais du XIVe siècle* (Paris, E. Leroux, 1899) vol. 2 (only one published).†

    Venture accounting; see Littleton and Yamey, p. 162, n. 12.

87. DUPONT, A., *Quelques documents et quelques ouvrages français antérieurs au règne de Louis XIII, ayant trait à la morale, à la doctrine et à la comptabilité commerciales*. (Paris, Société de Comptabilité de France, 1931) 55 pp.

    Accounting in France before the reign of Louis XIII (1610–43); includes a reproduction of the book-keeping section of Martin Fustel *L'Arithmétique abregée . . . Avec une briefue instruction pour secrettement escrire et tenir livres de raisons* (Paris, 1588).

88. FORESTIÉ, E. (ed.), *Les Livres de comptes des Frères Bonis, marchands montalbanais du XIVe siècle* (Paris, Honoré Champion, 1890 and 1893) vol. 1, ccxiii+243 pp.; vol. 2, vii+654 pp.

    'By far the most interesting French account-books of the Middle Ages' (R. de Roover in Littleton and Yamey, p. 161).

89. HOWARD, S. E., 'Public Rules for Private Accounting in France, 1673 and 1807', *Accounting Review*, VII (1932) 91–102, reprinted in MOONITZ, M. and LITTLETON, A. C., *Significant Accounting Essays* (Englewood Cliffs, N.J., Prentice-Hall, 1965) pp. 14–30.

    The effect on accounting of Louis XIV's *Ordinance* of 1673 and Napoleon's *Code de Commerce* of 1807.

90. MEYER, P., and GUIGUE, G., 'Fragments du grand livre d'un drapier de Lyon (1320–1323)', *Romania*, XXXV (1906) 428–44.

    The oldest extant French account book; in paragraph form.

91. MOLLAT, M., *Comptabilité du Port de Dieppe au XVe siècle* (Paris, Armand Colin, 1951) 139 pp.

    Reproduction of the port accounts with introduction.

92. SCHNEIDER, J., *Le livre de comptes des merciers messins Jean Le Clerc et Jacquemin de Moyeuvre (1460–1461)* (Metz, Librairie M. Mutelet, 1951) 105 pp.

    Includes a transcription of the account book.

93. WOLFF, PH., 'Une comptabilité commerciale du XVe siècle', *Annales du Midi*, LXIV (1952) 131–48.

    The accounts of Jean Lapeyre, merchant of Toulouse (in single entry).

F. EARLY ENGLISH AND SCOTTISH ACCOUNTING

(i) *Manorial, Household and Parochial Accounts*

94. BATHO, G. R. (ed.), *The Household Papers of Henry Percy, Ninth Earl of Northumberland (1564–1632)* (Camden 3rd ser, vol. 93, London, Royal Historical Society, 1962) lvii+190 pp.
    A reproduction of household accounts; interesting introduction.
95. COX, J. C., *Churchwardens' Accounts* (London, Methuen, 1913) 365 pp.
    Includes copious extracts from the accounts of many parishes.
95(a). DENHOLM-YOUNG, N., *Seignorial Administration in England* (Oxford University Press, 1937; London, Frank Cass, 1963) 196 pp.
    Includes a chapter on the system of account (pp. 120–61) and reproduces some *regule compoti* (in Latin) (pp. 169–76).
96. DREW, J. A., 'Manorial Accounts of St Swithun's Priory, Winchester', *English Historical Review*, LXII (1947) 20–41; reprinted in CARUS-WILSON, E. M., *Essays in Economic History*, 3 vols (London, Edward Arnold, 1962) II 12–30.
    Compares the financial relationship existing between the lord and the official in local charge of a manor as set out in such books as Walter of Henley's *Husbandry* (see item 104 on p. 90) and as in practice.
97. FOWLER, G. H., 'A Household Expense Roll, 1328', *English Historical Review*, LV (1940) 630–4.
    Includes a reproduction of the roll (in Latin).
98. GIBSON, S., 'The Oldest Account Book of the University of Oxford', *English Historical Review*, XXIV (1909) 735–43.
    The account book (in Latin) is reproduced; it records expenses incurred by university officials in connexion with journeys to London in 1357–8.
99. GRAS, N. S. B., and GRAS, E. C., *The Economic and Social History of an English Village (Crawley, Hampshire) A.D. 909–1928* (Cambridge, Mass., Harvard University Press, 1930) 730 pp.
    The first part of this book includes a discussion of manorial accounting (pp. 13–18); the second part includes reprints and translations of accounts.

100. HEATH, P., *Medieval Clerical Accounts* (York, St Anthony's Publications no. 26, 1964) 59 pp.

   The accounts of the vicarage and rectory of Hornsea, Yorkshire, in the late fifteenth century.

101. HONE, N. J., 'Account Rolls', pp. 203-23 of his *The Manor and Manorial Records* (London, Methuen, 1906).

   Includes many examples of manorial account rolls in translation.

102. JACK, S. M., 'An Historical Defence of Single Entry Bookkeeping', *Abacus*, II (1966) 137-58.

   Argues that medieval accounting was more efficient than is usually admitted.

103. JAMES, M. E. (ed.), *The Estate Accounts of The Earls of Northumberland, 1562-1637* (Publications of the Surtees Society, vol. 163, Durham, 1955).

   A reproduction of estate accounts; interesting introduction.

104. LAMOND, E. (ed.), *Walter of Henley's Husbandry, together with an anonymous Husbandry, Seneschaucie and Robert Grosseteste's rules* (London, Longmans, Green, 1890) 171 pp.

   These four medieval treatises are primarily concerned with general estate management but they also include much incidental information about manorial accounting.

105. LATHAM, R. E., 'Ministers' Accounts', *Amateur Historian*, I (1953) 112-17.

   A description of the method of accounting, including a reproduced text with translation.

106. *Legal and Manorial Formularies edited from originals at the British Museum and the Public Record Office in memory of Julius Parnell Gilson* (Oxford University Press, 1933) xviii+49 pp.

   The formularies include instructions for manorial accounting (in Latin, not translated).

107. LEVETT, A. E., 'The Financial Organization of the Manor', *Economic History Review*, 1st ser, I (1927) 65-86; reprinted in CAM, H. M., COATE, M., and SUTHERLAND, L. S. (eds), *Studies in Manorial History by Ada Elizabeth Levett* (Oxford University Press, 1938) pp. 41-68.

   Includes a discussion of manorial accounting.

108. MYATT-PRICE, E. M., 'Cromwell Household Accounts, 1417-1476', § pp. 99-113.

   The accounts studied consist of a day-book, a weekly book,

three annual accounts and a 'View of account'; they were kept by Lord Cromwell and members of his family at Tattershall Castle and at Tydd in Lincolnshire.

109. MYATT-PRICE, E. M., 'The Twelve at Tattershall', *Accounting Review*, XXXV (1960) 680–5.

Description of the household book recording the cost of maintaining a group of people at Tattershall Castle, Lincolnshire, in 1447 and 1448.

110. MYATT-PRICE, E. M., 'Examples of Techniques in Medieval Building Accounts', *Abacus*, II (1966) 41–8.

The object of the accounts was to clear the accountant in respect of receipts and expenditure for which he was personally responsible, not to provide evidence of profit or loss.

111. OSCHINSKY, D., 'Medieval Treatises on Estate Accounting', *Economic History Review*, 1st ser, XVII (1947) 52–61.§

A survey of the contemporary treatises on manorial accounting.

112. PAGE, F. M. (ed.), *Wellingborough Manorial Accounts A.D. 1258–1323 from the Account Rolls of Crowland Abbey* (Publications of the Northamptonshire Record Society, vol. 8, 1936; reprinted with note by T. H. Aston, 1965). Preface and Introduction xxxviii pp.; Text, Glossary and Indexes 144 pp.

The accounts are printed in Latin, some with a facing English translation. For extracts (with translation) from typical medieval accounts see GOODER, E. A., *Latin for Local History* (London, Longmans, Green, 1961) pp. 82–7.

113. READ, C., 'Lord Burghley's Household Accounts', *Economic History Review*, 2nd ser, IX (1956) 343–8.

Discusses an account book kept by Thomas Billot, steward of William Cecil, first Lord Burghley, for the years 1575–7.

114. SALZMAN, L. F. (ed.), *Ministers' Accounts of the Manor of Petworth 1347–1353* (Lewes, Sussex Record Society, vol. 55, 1955) Introduction pp. xxv–xxxiv, Translation etc. pp. 1–100.

Many ministers' accounts have been printed; this one has been chosen as an example because of the helpful introduction and because the accounts have been translated into English.

115. SIMPSON, A., 'Encounters with Accounts', pp. 1–21 of *The Wealth of the Gentry 1540–1660* (Chicago, University of Chicago Press, and London, Cambridge University Press, 1961) 226 pp.

A discussion of the problems of interpreting Tudor and Stuart household and manorial accounts.

116. SMITH, R. A. L., 'The Central Financial System of Christ Church, Canterbury, 1186–1512', *English Historical Review*, LV (1940) 353–369.

Includes a reprint of the Treasurer's Account for 1198–9.

117. STONE, E., 'Profit-and-Loss Accountancy at Norwich Cathedral Priory', *Transactions of the Royal Historical Society*, 5th ser, XII (1962) 25–48.

The author argues that some manorial accounting was aimed at profit measurement, not just at answering the question: 'Are we being cheated?'

118. TATE, W. E., *The Parish Chest* (Cambridge University Press, 3rd printing, 1960) 346 pp.

A study of the records of parochial administration in England; includes chapters on the accounts of churchwardens, charities and petty constables.

119. TUPLING, G. H., 'Searching the Parish Records', *Amateur Historian*, I (1953–54) 198–202, 234–7, 269–72, 301–4, 335–8, 361–4.

A series of articles which includes discussions of the accounts of churchwardens, overseers, highway surveyors and parish constables.

120. WOOD-LEGH, K. L. (ed.), *A Small Household of the XVth Century* (Manchester, University Press, 1956) xxxvi+90 pp.

The account book (in Latin) of Munden's Chantry, Bridport, Dorset.

(ii) *Mercantile Accounts*

121. BLAGDEN, C., 'A Bookseller's Memorandum Book, 1695–1720'. § pp. 255–65.

The account book of a Fleet Street bookseller.

122. BURLEY, K. H., 'Some Accounting Records of an Eighteenth-Century Clothier', *Accounting Research*, IX (1958) 50–60.

The rather primitive accounting records of Thomas Grigg of Ballingdon, Essex. There is some attempt at cost accounting.

123. CONNELL-SMITH, G. E., 'Ledger of Thomas Howell', *Economic History Review*, 2nd ser, III (1950), 363–70.

The oldest surviving ledger in English; covers the period 1517–28.
124. COOMBER, R. R., 'Hugh Oldcastle and John Mellis', *Accounting Research*, VII (1956) 201–16.§
Biographical information about Oldcastle and Mellis and a description of *A briefe instruction*. . . .
125. DANIELS, G. W., 'Trading Accounts of a London Merchant in 1794', *Economic Journal*, XXXIII (1923) 516–22.
The waste book and ledger of John Stubs for the period 1 Mar. to 31 Dec. 1794.
126. FRYDE, E. B., *The Wool Accounts of William de la Pole* (York, St Anthony's Press, 1964) 29 pp.
Selections (in Latin) from these early fourteenth-century accounts are reproduced.
127. GOLDBERG, L., 'Jeremy Bentham, Critic of Accounting Method', *Accounting Research*, VIII (1957) 218–45.
A study of Bentham's views on accounting.
128. GORDON, C., 'First English Books on Book-keeping', *Accounting Research*, V (1954) 215–18.§
Descriptions of the books by Oldcastle, Mellis, Ympyn, and Peele by a former Librarian of the Institute of Chartered Accountants in England and Wales.
129. HART, A. T., *Country Counting House* (London, Phoenix House, 1962) 142 pp.
The story of the eighteenth-century clerical account books of Squire Payne and Henry Mease.
130. HASSON, C. J., 'The South Sea Bubble and Mr Snell', *Journal of Accountancy*, LIV (1932) 128–37.
Discusses the Bubble and the early audit investigation 'Observations made upon examining the Books of Sawbridge and Company. By Charles Snell, Writing Master and Accomptant in Foster Lane, London' (1720).
131. HODGSON, R. A., 'An Early Accounting Textbook', *Accountancy*, LXVII (1956) 222–3.
A description of William Weston's *The Complete Merchant's Clerk, or British and American Counting House* (London, 1754, 1761, 1781).
132. HORNE, D. H., *The Life and Minor Works of George Peele* (New Haven, Conn., Yale University Press, 1952) 305 pp.

George Peele the Elizabethan dramatist was the son of James Peele, the writer of two books (1553 and 1569) on double entry. Chapter 1 of Horne's book is especially interesting to accountants.

133. INNES, C. (ed.), *Ledger of Andrew Halyburton, 1492-1503* (Edinburgh, Her Majesty's General Register House, 1867) cxvi+404 pp.

This ledger (not in double entry) was written up in the Netherlands. See also Ritson, F. A., 'Halyburton's Ledger and his Times', *Accountants' Magazine*, LXX (1966) 124-33.

134. KATS, P., 'De Invloed der Nederlanders der 16de en 17de eeuw op de Engelsche literatur van het Boekhouden', *Maanblad voor het Boekhouden*, XXXII (1925) 168-75.

Discusses the influence of the Netherlands in the sixteenth and seventeenth centuries on English book-keeping literature.

135. KATS, P., 'Double Entry Book-keeping in England before Hugh Oldcastle', *Accountant*, LXXIV (1926) 91-8.

Mainly concerned with the ledger of the Borromeo Company of London, 1436-9.

136. KATS, P., 'Hugh Oldcastle and John Mellis', *Accountant*, LXXIV (1926) 483-7, 641-8.

Includes an abridged version of Mellis's *Briefe Instruction*.

137. KATS, P., 'The "Nouuelle Instruction" of Jehan Ympyn Christophle', *Accountant*, LXXVII (1927) 261-9, 287-96.

Includes a reprint of the English version (1547) of Ympyn's book (in modern spelling).

138. KATS, P., 'James Peele's "Maner and Fourme"', *Accountant*, LXXXII (1930) 41-4, 88-91, 119-22.

Includes a reprint of Peele's book (1553) (in modern spelling).

139. LAPSLEY, C. T., 'Account Rolls of a Fifteenth Century Ironmaster', *English Historical Review*, vol. 14, pp. 509-29.

The roll (in bad Latin) is reproduced on pp. 516-29.

140. McGRATH, P. (ed.), *The Marchant Avizo by I[ohn] B[rown] Marchant, 1589* (Boston, Baker Library, Harvard Graduate School of Administration, 1957) Introduction xxxvi pp.; Text 64 pp.

A sixteenth-century manual for merchants; includes 'the forme of a Spanish accompt'.

SELECT BIBLIOGRAPHY 95

141. MILLAR, A. H. (ed.), *The Compt Buik of David Wedderburne, Merchant of Dundee 1587–1630* (Publications of the Scottish History Society, vol. 28, Edinburgh, 1898) lxxii+323 pp.
    The rather primitive accounting records of a Scottish merchant.

142. POLLARD, S., 'Capital Accounting in the Industrial Revolution', *Yorkshire Bulletin of Economic and Social Research*, XV (1963) 75–91.
    The growth of fixed capital in the Industrial Revolution did not lead to a general 'rationalisation' of accounting though the period 1770–1830 saw some advances towards it. See also 'Accounting and Management', ch. 6 of his *The Genesis of Modern Management* (London, Edward Arnold, 1965).

143. RAMSAY, G. D. (ed.), *John Isham, Mercer and Merchant Adventurer. Two Account Books of a London Merchant in the Reign of Elizabeth I* (Publications of the Northamptonshire Record Society, vol. 21, 1962) Preface and Introduction cxii pp.; Text, Appendixes and Indexes 197 pp.
    The nature and significance of the two ledgers reprinted are discussed on pp. c–cx of the Introduction. See also the review by Yamey in *Accountancy*, LXXIV (1963) 228.

144. RAMSEY, P., 'Some Tudor Merchants' Accounts',§ pp. 185–201.
    Discusses the surviving accounts of Thomas Howell, John Johnson, Thomas Laurence and Sir Thomas Gresham.

145. RICKERT, E., 'Extracts from a Fourteenth-Century Account Book', *Modern Philology*, XXIV (1926–7) 111–19, 249–56, partly reprinted in RICKERT, E., *Chaucer's World* (ed. Olson, C. C., and Crow, M. M.) (New York, Columbia University Press, 1948) pp. 185–93.
    The account book of Gilbert Maghfeld; see also James, M. K. 'A London Merchant of the Fourteenth Century', *Economic History Review*, 2nd ser, VIII (1956) 364–76.

146. SUTHERLAND, P. (pseudonym of COOMBER, R. R., and GORDON, C.), 'Hugh Oldcastle and the "Profitable Treatyce" of 1543', *Accountant*, CII (1940), 334–6.
    An account of the Oldcastle family; the disposition of a copy of Oldcastle's book and a copy of his will.

147. VANES, J., 'Sixteenth-Century Accounting. The Ledger of John Smythe, Merchant of Bristol', *Accountant*, CLVII (1967) 357–61.
    An example of venture accounting.

148. WALLACE, E. G., 'Accounting for Pirates', *Chartered Secretary*, VI (1966) 437-40.

Discusses Thomas Dilworth's *The Young Book-keeper's Assistant* (London, new ed., 1854).

149. YAMEY, B. S., 'Edward Jones's "English System of Book-keeping"', *Accounting Review*, XIX (1944) 407-16.

Jones's *The English System of Book-keeping* (Bristol, 1796) and the reactions of the supporters of the 'Italian method'.

150. YAMEY, B. S., 'Edward Jones and the Reform of Book-keeping 1795-1810', § pp. 313-24.

More about Jones and the reactions to his book.

151. YAMEY, B. S., 'Early Books on Accounting: Carpenter's *Most Excellent Instruction* (1632) and Other Works', *Accountant*, CXXXVII (1957) 683-4.

Carpenter's book is borrowed mainly from Waninghen (1615), Peele (1553), Mellis (1588) and Buingha (1627).

152. YAMEY, B. S., 'Handson's *Analysis of Merchants' Accompts* - An Unrecorded Broadside, 1669', *Accounting Research*, VIII (1957) 299-304.

A discussion of Handson's 'broadside' (single printed sheet).

153. YAMEY, B. S., 'Handson's *Analysis of Merchants' Accompts* - A Further Note', *Accounting Research*, IX (1958) 61-2.

Further discussion of Handson's broadside.

154. YAMEY, B. S., 'Weddington's *A Breffe Instruction*, 1567', *Accounting Research*, IX (1958) 124-33.

A discussion of Weddington's book.

155. YAMEY, B. S., 'Stephen Monteage. A Seventeenth-Century Accountant', *Accountancy*, LXX (1959) 594-5.

Monteage as practical accountant and textbook-writer.

156. YAMEY, B. S., 'Some Topics in the History of Financial Accounting in England 1500-1900', in BAXTER, W. T., and DAVIDSON, S. (eds), *Studies in Accounting Theory* (London, Sweet & Maxwell, 1962) pp. 14-43.

Discusses (i) accounts not on a double-entry basis, (ii) the early practice of double entry (1500-1800), (iii) the calculation of profit in the accounts of joint-stock companies.

157. YAMEY, B. S., 'John Jones's *Diarium Mercatoris*. An Eighteenth-Century Exposition of Accounting', *Accountancy*, LXXVII (1966) 544-6.

Jones's exposition was incorporated (without acknowledgement) in Postlethwayt's *Universal Dictionary of Trade and Commerce* (1751).

158. YAMEY, B. S., EDEY, H. C., and THOMSON, H. W., *Accounting in England and Scotland: 1543–1800* (London, Sweet & Maxwell, 1963) 228 pp.

Part One contains over a hundred extracts from thirty-one books on accounting up to the year 1800 together with one from 1818. Part Two contains (i) a survey of the books in English up to 1800, (ii) a discussion of double entry in practice in the seventeenth and eighteenth centuries (largely a combination of two articles by Yamey in *Accounting Review*, XXXIV (1959) 534–46, and *Accountancy*, LXXI (1960) 639–41), and (iii) a bibliography of books on accounting in English, 1543–1800.

(iii) *Government Accounts*

159. ARMET, H., 'Mr Treasurer, Edinburgh – before 1835', *Local Government Finance*, vol. 60, pp. 140–2, 169–70.

Several similar articles have been published in the same journal.

160. HALCROW, E. M., 'Chamberlain's or Treasurer's Accounts', *Amateur Historian*, II (1956) 293–6.

A useful short discussion.

161. HALL, H., *The Antiquities and Curiosities of the Exchequer* (London, Elliot Stock, 1891) xviii+230 pp.

A study of 'the earliest and greatest counting-house in the kingdom' (p. xi).

162. JENKINSON, H., and BROOME, D. M., 'An Exchequer Statement of Receipts and Issues 1339–1340', *English Historical Review*, LVIII (1943) 210–16.

Most of this article is a discussion of the nature of medieval accounting.

163. JOHNSON, C. (trans. and ed.), *Dialogus de Scaccario* (London, Nelson, 1950) lxiv+144 pp.

The *Dialogus de Scaccario* of Richard, son of Nigel, Treasurer of England and Bishop of London, was written in the late twelfth century. It is a detailed practical treatise on the accounting methods of the English Exchequer.

164. KELLY, J. P., 'The Audit of Government Accounts in Britain', *Accounting Research*, VII (1956) 42–51.
   The development of the British system of parliamentary supervision over public expenditure.
165. LIVOCK, D. M., 'The Accounts of the Corporation of Bristol, 1532 to 1835', *Journal of Accounting Research*, III (1965) 86–102.
   A discussion of the accounting methods employed by the corporation.
166. LIVOCK, D. M. (ed.), *City Chamberlains' Accounts in the Sixteenth and Seventeenth Centuries* (Bristol Record Society, vol. 24, 1966).
167. NORMANTON, E. L., *The Accountability and Audit of Governments* (Manchester, University Press, and New York, Praeger, 1966) 452 pp.
   The first two chapters (pp. 1–27) are mainly historical.
168. PARSLOE, G. (ed.), *Wardens' Accounts of the Worshipful Company of Founders of the City of London 1497–1681* (Athlone Press, University of London, 1964) lviii+491 pp.
   Charge and discharge accounting.
169. POOLE, R. L., *The Exchequer in the Twelfth Century* (Oxford, Clarendon Press, 1912) 195 pp.
   Discusses such topics as the *Dialogus de Scaccario* (see Johnson above), pipe rolls (see Stenton below), tallies (see Robert below) and the use of the abacus.
170. ROBERT, R., 'A Short History of Tallies', *Accounting Research*, III (1952) 220–9.§
   Based partly on the articles by Sir Hilary Jenkinson in *Archaeologia*, LXII (1911) 367–80, *Proceedings of the Society of Antiquaries*, 2nd ser, XXV (1913) 29–39, and *Archaeologia*, LXXIV (1925) 289–351. Tallies continued to be used until 1826.
171. STENTON, D. M. (ed.), *The Great Roll of the Pipe for the Second Year of the Reign of King Richard the First* (London, Publications of the Pipe Roll Society, vol. 39, N.S. vol. 1, 1925) xxv+239 pp.
   This is the pipe roll containing the accounts from Michaelmas 1189 to Michaelmas 1190. This volume has been selected for inclusion because of the valuable introduction (pp. xiii–xxv) by Charles Johnson.
172. WOLFFE, B. P., 'The Management of English Royal Estates under the Yorkist Kings', *English Historical Review*, LXXI (1956) 1–27.
   Contains many references to accounting and auditing.

173. WREN, M. C., 'The Chamber of the City of London', *Accounting Review*, XXIV (1949) 191–8.
 Based on the City account books; see also Wren's article in *Economic History Review*, 2nd ser, 1 (1948) 46–53.

G. EARLY IRISH ACCOUNTING

174. FREEMAN, A. M. (transcriber), *The Compossicion Booke of Conought* (Dublin Stationery Office for Irish Manuscripts Commission, 1936) ix+179 pp.
175. LONGFIELD, A. K. (ed.), *The Shapland Carew Papers* (Dublin Stationery Office, 1946) x+228 pp.
 Eighteenth- and nineteenth-century household accounts.
176. LONGFIELD, A. K. (ed.), *Fitzwilliam Accounts 1560–65 (Annesley Collection)* (Dublin Stationery Office for the Irish Manuscripts Commission, 1960) xii+139 pp.
 Government accounting in sixteenth-century Ireland.

H. EARLY GERMAN AND AUSTRIAN ACCOUNTING

177. DENUCÉ, J., *Die Hanse und die Antwerpener Handelskompanien in den Ostseeländern* (Antwerp, De Sikkel, 1938) 160 pp.
 Includes a voyage account, 1573–6, and the journal of a voyage from Stockholm to Riga, 1562–5.
178. PENNDORF, B., *Geschichte der Buchhaltung in Deutschland* (Leipzig, Gloeckner, 1913) 248 pp.
179. PICKL, O., *Des Älteste Geschäftsbuch Österreichs* (Graz, Verlag der Historischen Landeskommission, 1966) 495 pp.
 A detailed study of the surviving account books of the firm of Alexius Funck (of Wiener Neustadt) for the period 1516–*c*. 1538.

180. STEVELINCK, E. and HAULOTTE, R., 'Early Book-keeping in Germany', *Accountants' Magazine*, LXXI (1967), 393–6. Discusses Heinrich Schreiber's *Ayn New Künstlich Buech*... (1518).
181. STRIEDER, J., *Die Inventur der Firma Fugger aus dem Jahre 1527* (Tübingen, Verlag der H. Laupp'schen Buchhandlung, 1905) 127 pp.
182. THIERFELDER, H. (ed.), *Rostock-Osloer Handelsbeziehungen im 16. Jahrhundert. Die Geschäftspapiere der Kaufleute Kron in Rostock und Bene in Oslo* (Weimar, Hermann Böhlaus Nachfolger, 1958) 256 pp. Includes the accounts of merchants at Rostock and Oslo who traded with each other, 1544–64.
183. TREMEL, L. F., *Das Handelsbuch des Judenburger Kaufmannes Clemens Körbler 1526–1548* (Graz, Beiträge zur Erforschung steirischer Geschichtsquellen XLVII. Heft, 1960) xxxix+127 pp. Reproduces Körbler's account book.
184. WEITNAUER, A., *Venetianischer Handel der Fugger nach der Musterbuchhaltung des Matthäus Schwarz* (Munich and Leipzig, Duncker & Humblot, 1931) xvi+323 pp. A reproduction with lengthy introduction of a sixteenth-century German manuscript on book-keeping. The manuscript is also discussed in Penndorf, *Geschichte der Buchaltung in Deutschland* (item 178 above); by Yamey in *Journal of Accounting Research*, Spring 1967 (item 36 above); and by M. L. Hartsough, 'A New Treatise on Book-keeping under the Fuggers', *Journal of Economic and Business History*, IV (1931) 539–51.

I. EARLY AMERICAN ACCOUNTING

185. BAXTER, W. T., *House of Hancock* (Cambridge, Mass., Harvard University Press, 1945, and New York, Russell & Russell, 1965) xxvii+321 pp. An eighteenth-century Boston merchant house as revealed by its account books.

SELECT BIBLIOGRAPHY 101

186. BAXTER, W. T., 'Credits, Bills and Book-keeping in a Simple Economy', *Accounting Review*, XXI (1946) 154-66; reprinted in W. T. BAXTER (ed.), *Studies in Accounting* (London, Sweet & Maxwell, 1950) pp. 31-48.
    The relationship between credit and accounting in eighteenth-century America.
187. BAXTER, W. T., 'Accounting in Colonial America',§ pp. 272-87.
    Further information on credit, barter and book-keeping in colonial America.
188. BRUCHEY, S. W., *Robert Oliver, Merchant of Baltimore 1783-1819* (Baltimore, Johns Hopkins University Studies in Historical and Political Science, LXXIV i (1956)) 411 pp.
    Accounting methods and their relation to investment decisions are discussed on pp. 135-41.
189. HOWARD, S. E., 'Charge and Discharge', *Accounting Review*, VI (1931) 51-6.
    A description of Thomas Turner's *An Epitome of Book-keeping by Double Entry* (Portland, Mass., 1804).
190. JENNINGS, R. M., 'Selections from a Pre-Revolutionary Accounting Record', *Accounting Review*, XXXVII (1962) 73-5.
    The account book of a Rhode Island firm in the early eighteenth century.
191. VOKE, A. J., 'Accounting Methods of Colonial Merchants in Virginia', *Journal of Accountancy*, XLII (1926) 1-11.
    The merchants' account books gave details of debtors and creditors, profit or loss on each activity and property owned.

J. EARLY AUSTRALIAN ACCOUNTING

192. GODDARD, R. H., 'An Historical Survey', *Chartered Accountant in Australia*, VIII (1938) 681-97.
    Includes reprints of 'An account of the expense incurred in transporting convicts to New South Wales, as far as the same can be made up' and of the first balance sheets of the Australian Agricultural Company (31 Dec. 1833) and of the Bank of New South Wales (31 Dec. 1825).

193. GOLDBERG, L., 'Some Early Australian Accounting Records', *Australian Accountant*, XXII (1952) 346-55.§
Nineteenth-century accounting records in the Mitchell Library, Sydney. None of them are in double entry.
194. MCCREDIE, H., 'Early Accounting Records - The University of Sydney, 1851-1861', *Bulletin of the Business Archives Council of Australia*, I iv (1958) 12-19.
The accounts of the University of Sydney have been kept in double entry since its inception in 1851.
195. MCCREDIE, H., 'An early Ledger of the Firm Messrs Cooper & Levey, 1823-5', *Bulletin of the Business Archives Council of Australia*, I vii (1960) 19-41.
The ledger was not kept in double entry; several of the accounts are reproduced in the article.
196. MACMILLAN, D. S., and MCCREDIE, H., 'Accounting for a Scottish Venture in Colonial Development', *Bulletin of the Business Archives Council of Australia*, I ix (1961) 66-83.
The accounting records of the Scottish Australian Company mainly in the 1840's; they were kept in double entry.

K. EARLY JAPANESE ACCOUNTING

197. FUJITA, Y., 'The Evolution of Financial Reporting in Japan', *International Journal of Accounting*, II (1966) 49-75.
Japanese financial reporting since c. 1870 with special reference to the related legal background.
198. NISHIKAWA, K., 'The Early History of Double-Entry Book-keeping in Japan',§ pp. 380-7.
After the opening up of Japan to foreign influence in 1854, modern book-keeping was imported simultaneously from several countries.
199. NISHIKAWA, K., *Introduction of Double-Entry Book-keeping to Japan by Vicente E. Braga in 1870s* (Tokyo, Moriyama Book Store, 1960) 22 pp. in English+17 pp. in Japanese.
Details of Braga and his rôle in introducing double entry into Japan.

200. SHIMME, S., 'Introduction of Double-Entry Book-keeping into Japan', *Accounting Review*, XII (1937) 290-5.
   The technique of double entry was introduced into Japan about 1865; the first book on the subject in Japanese (a translation of an American book) was published in 1873.

L. EARLY INDIAN ACCOUNTING

201. KULSHRESTHA, H. S., 'The Inventors of Modern Accounting', *Chartered Accountant* (India), IX (1961) 418-20.
   The case for an Indian origin of double entry.

M. PROFESSIONAL ACCOUNTANCY

202. ARTHUR ANDERSEN & CO., *The First Fifty Years 1913-1963* (Chicago, Arthur Andersen & Co., 1963) 201 pp.
   An example of a history of an American accountancy firm.
203. ASSOCIATION OF CERTIFIED AND CORPORATE ACCOUNTANTS, *Fifty Years – The Story of the Association of Certified and Corporate Accountants 1904-54* (London, Association of Certified and Corporate Accountants, 1954) 70 pp.
   An official history.
204. AUSTRALIAN SOCIETY OF ACCOUNTANTS, *History of the Australian Society of Accountants and its Antecedent Bodies 1887 to 1962* (Melbourne, Australian Society of Accountants, 1964) 93 pp.
   Does not repeat the detail given in the separate histories of the antecedent Commonwealth and Federal Institutes (see below).
205. CASLER, D. J., *The Evolution of C.P.A. Ethics: A Profile of Professionalization* (East Lansing, Bureau of Business and Economic Research, Michigan State University, 1964) 139 pp.
   Traces the evolution of the various rules and notes the social forces behind their development.

206. COMMONWEALTH INSTITUTE OF ACCOUNTANTS, 'Historical Survey 1886–1930', in *Commonwealth Accountants' Year Book 1936* (Melbourne, Commonwealth Institute of Accountants, 1936) pp. 5–55.

The first fifty years of the oldest of the antecedent bodies of the Australian Society of Accountants.

207. COOPER BROTHERS & Co., *A History of Cooper Brothers & Co. 1854 to 1954* (London, privately published for Cooper Brothers & Co., by B. T. Batsford Ltd., 1954) 116 pp.

An example of a history of a British accountancy firm. See also COOPER, E., 'Fifty-Seven Years in an Accountant's Office', *Accountant*, LXV (1921) 553–63.

208. DIEN, E. VAN, 'The Development of Professional Accounting in Continental Europe', *Accountant*, LXXXI (1929) 409–17, 439–48.

The countries considered are: Austria, Belgium, Czechoslovakia, Denmark, Finland, France, Germany, Italy, the Netherlands, Norway, Poland, Romania, Russia, Sweden and Switzerland.

209. EDWARDS, J. D., *History of Public Accounting in the United States* (East Lansing, Michigan State University, 1961) 368 pp.

The author states that the 'emphasis is less on interpretation of events than on the events themselves' (p. 2).

210. GARRETT, A. A., *History of the Society of Incorporated Accountants 1885–1957* (printed at the University Press, Oxford, 1961) 360 pp.

Written by the Secretary of the Society, 1919–49. The Society was amalgamated with the Chartered Institutes of the United Kingdom in 1957.

211. GRADY, P. (ed.), *Memoirs and Accounting Thought of George O. May* (New York, Ronald, 1962) 313 pp.

The memoirs and opinions of an English chartered accountant who became a leader of the profession in the United States.

212. GRAHAM, A. W., *First Fifty Years, 1909–1959* (Wellington, New Zealand Society of Accountants, 1960) 152 pp.

Written by the Secretary of the New Zealand Society.

213. HAERNING, M., 'The Profession in Denmark. Origin, Development and Present Day Activities', *Accountant*, CXXXIII (1955) 181–5.

A short survey.

214. INSTITUTE OF CHARTERED ACCOUNTANTS OF SCOTLAND, *A History of the Chartered Accountants of Scotland from the Earliest Times to 1954*

(Edinburgh, Institute of Chartered Accountants of Scotland, 1954) 183 pp.

The history of the oldest existing accountancy body in the world.

215. INSTITUTE OF CHARTERED ACCOUNTANTS IN ENGLAND AND WALES, *The History of The Institute of Chartered Accountants in England and Wales 1880–1965 and of its founder accountancy bodies 1870–1880* (London, Heinemann, 1966) 269 pp.

The official history of the largest professional body of accountants in the United Kingdom.

216. JEAL, E. F., 'Some Reflections on the Evolution of the Professional Practice of Accountancy in Great Britain', *Accountant*, XCVI (1937) 521–8.

A general survey stressing the need for public confidence.

217. KRAAYENHOF, J., 'The Profession in the Netherlands. Sixty Years of Growth and Development', *Accountant*, CXXXIII (1955) 382–90.

The story of the Nederlands Instituut van Accountants (founded 1895).

218. MASKELL, R. E., 'Fifty Years of Accountancy Progress. The History of the Federal Institute of Accountants 1894–1944', *Federal Accountant*, XXVI (1944) 201–51.

The first fifty years of one of the antecedent bodies of the Australian Society of Accountants.

219. MURPHY, M. E., 'Arthur Lowes Dickinson: Pioneer in American Professional Accountancy', *Bulletin of the Business Historical Society*, XXI (1947) 27–38.

A short biography of an English chartered accountant who practised in the United States, 1901–11; see also the same author's articles in *The Accountant*, CXVII (1947).

220. MURPHY, M. E., 'Notes on Accounting History', *Accounting Research*, I (1950) 275–80.

Mainly a bibliographical survey of the history of professional accountancy. See also the same author's 'Recent Research in British Accounting History', *Business History Review*, XXIX (1955) 263–76.

221. MURPHY, M. E., 'The Victorian Age of Accountancy', *Chartered Accountant in Australia*, XXV (1954) 131–40.

Professional accountancy in Victorian Britain.

222. MURPHY, M. E., 'Heritage of the American Accounting Profession' and 'Founding Fathers of the American Accounting Profession', chs 1 and 2, pp. 1-34 of her *Advanced Public Accounting Practice* (Homewood, Ill., Irwin, 1966).

A well-documented short account of the beginnings of professional accountancy in the United States.

223. NOYCE, G. E., 'History of the Profession in South Africa', *South African Accountant*, 1 (1954) 3-12.

From the early European settlements to registration of the South African profession in 1951.

224. PARKER, R. H., 'Australia's Oldest Accountancy Body - The Adelaide Society of Accountants', *Chartered Accountant in Australia*, XXXII (1961) 337-40.

The Adelaide Society of Accountants was the oldest of the antecedent bodies of the Institute of Chartered Accountants in Australia. No history of the Australian Institute has yet been written.

225. POYNTON, T. L., *The Institute of Municipal Treasurers and Accountants. A Short History 1885-1960* (London, Institute of Municipal Treasurers and Accountants, 1960) 166 pp.

A well-written account of the first seventy-five years of a specialised accountancy body.

226. ROBINSON, H. W., *A History of Accountants in Ireland* (Dublin, Institute of Chartered Accountants in Ireland, 1964) 485 pp.

Mainly the story of two accountancy bodies which like many others were 'born through bankruptcies, fed on failures and frauds, grew on liquidations and graduated through audits' (p. 30). Of more than parochial interest.

227. STACEY, N. A. H., *English Accountancy: A Study in Social and Economic History, 1800-1954* (London, Gee, 1954) 295 pp.

A critical survey by a non-accountant.

228. WORTHINGTON, B., *Professional Accountants: an Historical Sketch* (London, Gee, 1895) 127 pp.

An early British work which is still of interest.

N. AUDITING

229. BOUTELL, W. S., 'Auditing in a Changing Environment', pp. 46–59 of his *Auditing with the Computer* (Berkeley and Los Angeles, University of California Press, 1965).
   Mainly concerned with twentieth-century developments, especially internal control.
230. BROWN, R. G., 'Changing Audit Objectives and Techniques', *Accounting Review*, XXXVII (1962) 696–703.
   Increased reliance on internal controls and a decrease in detailed testing are the most important changes.
231. COCHRANE, G., 'The Auditor's Report. Its Evolution in the U.S.A.', *Accountant*, CXXIII (1950) 448–60, reprinted in MURPHY, M. E. (ed.), *Selected Readings in Accounting and Auditing* (New York, Prentice-Hall, 1952).
   A short general account which includes seven forms of report from the period 1915–49.
232. HAULOTTE, R., 'La révision comptable à travers les âges', pp. 23–33 of COLLEYE, J., DEFAT, A. and HAULOTTE, R., *Introduction à la Révision Comptable* (Brussels, Éditions Comptabilité et Productivité, n.d.).
   A short survey of auditing history.
233. HEIN, L. W., 'The Auditor and the British Companies Acts', *Accounting Review*, XXXVIII (1963) 508–20.
   A survey of the influence of company legislation on auditing in Britain, 1844–1963.
234. LEWIS, N. B., 'A Certificate of the Earl of Lancaster's Auditors', *English Historical Review*, LV (1940) 99–103.
   An example of a medieval audit certificate (in Latin).
235. MOYER, C. A., 'Early Developments in American Auditing', *Accounting Review*, XXVI (1951) 3–8, reprinted in JOHNSON, J. T., and BRASSEAUX, J. H., *Readings in Auditing* (Cincinnati, South-Western, 1960) pp. 2–9.
   Auditing in the United States in the late nineteenth and early twentieth centuries.
236. POLLINS, H., 'Railway Auditing – A Report of 1867', *Accounting Research*, VIII (1957) 14–22.
   The report issued by the two auditors of the London & North-Western Railway in 1867.

237. STAUB, W. A., *Auditing Developments during the Present Century* (Cambridge, Mass., Harvard University Press, 1942) 99 pp.
A survey by a participant in the developments in the United States.

O. COST AND MANAGEMENT ACCOUNTING

238. AMODEO, D., 'The Development of Modern Cost Accounting in Italy', *N.A.C.A. Bulletin*, XXVI (1945) 855–62.
The period covered is 1927–45.
239. ASTON, C. W., 'There is No New Thing... An Early Treatise on Accounting for Management', *Accountant*, CXXXV (1956) 512–13.
See also 'Victorian Venture', *Economist*, CXCVII (1960) 1327–8.
240. BARTON, A. D., 'The Break-Even Chart', *Australian Accountant*, XXVI (1956) 375–88.
The first part of this article analyses the early development of the break-even chart.
241. BRUMMET, R. LEE, 'Brief History of Overhead Costing since 1875', pp. 1–13 of his *Overhead Costing* (Ann Arbor, Michigan Business Studies, XIII ii (1957)).
242. CHAPIN, N., 'The Development of the Break-Even Chart: A Bibliographical Note', *Journal of Business*, XXVIII (1955) 148–9.
The break-even chart derives from the work of Henry Hess at the beginning of the twentieth century.
243. CROSSMAN, P., 'The Genesis of Cost Control', *Accounting Review* XXVIII (1953) 522–7.
Cost control as discussed by Hamilton (1788), Babbage (1832), Gibson (1887), Norton (1891), Mann (1891), Garcke and Fells (4th ed., 1893), Plumpton (1892) and Slater Lewis (1896).
244. DE CAZAUX, L. F. G., 'On the Budget', *Journal of Accounting Research*, III (1965) 264–5.
A translation of book II, chapter II of de Cazaux's *Éléments d'Économie Privée et Publique* (Paris, 1825).
245. DE ROOVER, Florence Edler, 'Cost Accounting in the Sixteenth Century', *Accounting Review*, XII (1937) 226–37; reprinted in

SOLOMONS, D. (ed.), *Studies in Costing* (London, Sweet & Maxwell, 1952) pp. 53–71.
> A description of the cost-accounting system of the Antwerp publisher, printer and bookseller Christopher Plantin.

246. DE ROOVER, R., 'A Florentine Firm of Cloth Manufacturers', *Speculum*, XVI (1941) 3–33.
> Cost accounting by the Medici in sixteenth-century Florence.

247. EDWARDS, R. S., *Survey of the French Contributions to the Study of Cost Accounting during the Nineteenth Century* (London, Gee, 1937; also published as supplement to *Accountant*, XCVI (1937) 1–37.)
> Deals with the work of Payen; double-entry manufacturing accounts; industrial and agricultural uses of cost accounts.

248. EDWARDS, R. S., 'Some Notes on the Early Literature and Development of Cost Accounting in Great Britain', *Accountant*, XCVII (1937) 193–5, 225–31, 253–5, 283–7, 313–16, and 343–4.
> Problems of costing in particular industries and a discussion of the treatment of oncost. An illustrated survey of the literature.

249. GARNER, S. P., *Evolution of Cost Accounting to 1925* (Alabama, University of Alabama Press, 1954) 416 pp.
> The standard work on the history of cost accounting. Extensive bibliography.

250. HEIN, L. W., 'J. Lee Nicholson: Pioneer Cost Accountant', *Accounting Review*, XXXIV (1959) 106–11.
> A short biography.

251. JACKSON, J. H., 'A Half-Century of Cost Accounting Progress', *N.A.C.A. Bulletin*, XXXIV (1952) 3–17; reprinted in THOMAS, W. E. (ed.), *Readings in Cost Accounting, Budgeting and Control* (Cincinnati, South-Western, 2nd ed., 1960) pp. 15–28.
> A brief survey of cost accounting in the first half of the twentieth century, with particular reference to the period 1920–52.

252. LITTLETON, A. C., 'Old and New in Management and Accounting', *Accounting Review*, XXIX (1954) 196–200, reprinted in MOONITZ, M. and LITTLETON, A. C. (eds), *Significant Accounting Essays* (Englewood Cliffs, N.J., Prentice-Hall, 1965) pp. 31–7.
> Management accounting practices in the household of a Tudor nobleman.

253. MARPLE, R. P., 'Historical Background', pp. 3–14 of his *National Association of Accountants on Direct Costing: Selected Papers* (New York, Ronald, 1965).
　　A short account of the evolution of direct costing.
254. MATTESICH, R., 'On the Evolution of Budgeting and Budget Simulation', ch. 2, pp. 5–10 of his *Simulation of the Firm through a Budget Computer Program* (Homewood, Ill., Irwin, 1964).
　　From J. O. McKinsey's *Budgetary Control* (1922) to the early 1960's.
255. MOST, K. S., 'The history of uniform cost accounting', pp. 40–8 of his *Uniform Cost Accounting* (London, Gee, 1961).
　　Mainly concerned with developments in the United Kingdom.
256. NIELSEN, O., 'A Predecessor of Direct Costing', *Journal of Accounting Research*, IV (1966) 119–20.
　　An anticipation of direct costing in South Dakota in 1919.
257. RAYMOND, R. H., 'History of the Flexible Budget', *Management Accounting* (U.S.A.), XLVII (1966) 9–15.
　　A short survey of the historical background.
258. ROGERS, D. M., 'Development of the Modern Business Budget', *Journal of Accountancy*, LIII (1932) 186–205.
　　Deals mainly with American developments in the first third of the twentieth century.
259. SCORGIE, M. B., 'Rate of Return', *Abacus*, 1 i (1965) 85–91.
　　Discusses the contribution of Alfred Marshall, A. M. Wellington and Joel Dean.
260. SIZER, J., 'The Development of Marginal Costing', *Accountants' Magazine*, LXXII (1968) 23–30.
　　Examines history in order to understand the obstructions which have delayed the general acceptance of marginal costing.
260(a). SMITH, M., 'An Historical Perspective', *N.A.A. Bulletin*, vol. 40, no. 11, sec. 2 (1959) pp. 3–12.
　　The first forty years of the National Association of (Cost) Accountants.
261. SOLOMONS, D., 'The Historical Development of Costing' in SOLOMONS, D. (ed.), *Studies in Costing* (London, Sweet & Maxwell, 1952) pp. 1–52.
　　The best short survey of the subject.

262. STEPHENS, R. J., 'A Note on an Early Reference to Cost-Volume-Profit Relationships', *Abacus*, II i (1966) 78–83.
    The reference is in A. M. WELLINGTON's *Economic Theory of the Location of Railways* (3rd ed., 1888).
263. THEISS, E. L., 'The Beginnings of Business Budgeting', *Accounting Review*, XII (1937) 43–55.
    Traces the influence of governmental budgeting and industrial engineering on the growth of business budgets.
264. VILLERS, R., 'The Origin of the Break-Even Chart', *Journal of Business*, XXVIII (1955) 296–7.
    Stresses the contribution of Walter Rautenstrauch.
265. WEBER, K., *Amerikanische Standardkostenrechnung* (Winterthur, Keller, 1960) 380 pp.
    A survey of the development of standard costing in the United States. Has not been translated into English.
266. WEBER, C., *The Evolution of Direct Costing* (Urbana, Ill., Center for International Education and Research in Accounting, 1966) 117 pp.
    A well-documented discussion of its subject; good bibliography.
267. WING, G. A., 'Capital Budgeting, Circa 1915', *Journal of Finance*, XX (1965) 472–9.
    Discusses an article by John Van Deventer in *American Machinist*, vol. 42, 1915.
268. WRIGHT, F. K., 'The British Army Cost Accounting Experiment', *Australian Accountant*, XXVI (1956) 463–70.
    The author claims that what failed was not an accounting system but an attempt to decentralise the administration of the British Army.

P. CORPORATE ACCOUNTING

269. ANTON, H. R., 'Funds Statement Forms and Presentation', pp. 45–64 of his *Accounting for the Flow of Funds* (Boston, Houghton Mifflin, 1962).
    Traces the development of the funds statement since W. M. Cole's 'Where-Got Where-Gone' statement of 1915.

270. BUTTIMER, H., 'The Evolution of Stated Capital', *Accounting Review*, XXXVII (1962) 746–52.

　　The development of the stated capital concept in the United States.

271. CLAIRE, R. S., 'Evolution of Corporate Reports', *Journal of Accountancy*, LXXIX (1945) 39–51.

　　A review of the progress in the art of financial reporting 1901–1943 as revealed by the reports of the United States Steel Corporation.

272. EDEY, H. C., 'Company Accounting in the Nineteenth and Twentieth Centuries', *Accountant's Journal* (U.K.) XLVIII (1956) 95–6, 127–9.

　　From the Joint Stock Companies Act of 1844 to the Companies Act of 1948.

273. EDEY, H. C., and PANITPAKDI, PROT, 'British Company Accounting and the Law 1844–1900', § pp. 356–79.

　　The salient features of British company-accounting law in the nineteenth century.

274. GREGORY, R. H., and WALLACE, E. L., 'Solution of Funds Statement Problems – History and Proposed New Method', *Accounting Research*, III (1952) 99–132.

　　Reviews the history of the word 'funds' and traces the history of methods for solving funds statement problems.

275. HAWKINS, D. F., 'The Development of Modern Financial Reporting Practices among American Manufacturing Corporations', *Business History Review*, XXXVII (1963) 135–68.

　　The movement away from nineteenth-century traditions of corporate secrecy towards the disclosure of the mid-twentieth.

276. JONES, F. H., 'Fifty Years of Company Accounts', *Accountant's Journal* (U.K.) XLVI (1954) 377–80.

　　Includes a comparison of the Balance Sheet of Lever Brothers Ltd at 31 Dec. 1903, and the Consolidated Balance Sheets of Unilever Ltd and Unilever N.V. and their Subsidiaries at 31 Dec. 1953.

277. KÄFER, K., and ZIMMERMAN, V. K., 'Notes on the Evolution of the Statement of Sources and Application of Funds', *International Journal of Accounting*, II (1967) 89–121.

　　A well-documented survey dealing with British and European as well as American developments.

278. STRICKETT, H. E., 'History of and Developments in the Presentation of Accounts', *Accountant's Journal* (N.Z.) XXXVIII (1960) 248–252.
    Mainly concerned with New Zealand developments; includes a reprint of the balance sheet of the Auckland Gas Co. Ltd 'for the year ending 10 July, 1863' (*sic*).

279. YAMEY, B. S., 'The Development of Company Accounting Conventions', *Three Banks Review*, no. 47 (1960) pp. 22–37; *Accountants' Magazine*, LXV (1961) 753–63.
    The present accounting conventions are essentially the product of the second half of the nineteenth century, and can be attributed to the growth in the number and importance of joint stock companies.

280. 'Companies and their Accounts. Peninsular and Oriental in 1904 and Now', *Accountant's Journal* (U.K.) XLVI (1954) 369–72.
    A comparison of the published P. and O. accounts for 1903–4 and 1952–3.

Q. MECHANISED ACCOUNTING AND COMPUTERS

281. BOUTELL, W. S., 'The Development of the Business-Oriented Computer', pp. 23–45 of his *Auditing with the Computer* (Berkeley and Los Angeles, University of California Press, 1965).
    Mainly concerned with events since 1944.

282. BOWDEN, B. V., 'A Brief History of Computation', ch. 1, pp. 3–31 of Bowden, B. V. (ed.), *Faster than Thought* (London, Pitman, 1953).
    Mainly concerned with the contributions of Charles Babbage.

283. FITZPATRICK, R. J., 'From Shadrach to Univac', *Data Processing*, III (1961) 24–8.
    Traces the development through clay, papyrus and paper to electronic data processing.

284. MCRAE, T. W., 'The History of EDP', pp. 34–49 of his *The Impact of Computers on Accounting* (London, Wiley, 1964).
    From ENIAC to the present.

285. MORRISON, P., and MORRISON, E., *Charles Babbage and his Calculating Engines* (New York, Dover Publications, 1961) xxxviii+ 400 pp.
    Includes extracts from Babbage's autobiography and from his writings on 'calculating engines'.

R. EXECUTORSHIP ACCOUNTING

286. HAY, L. E., 'Executorship Reporting – Some Historical Notes', *Accounting Review*, XXXVI (1961) 100–4.
    Examples of (mainly) early English and American executorship reports.
287. MONTGOMERIE, A., 'An East Lothian Executor's Accounts 1645–1650', *Scottish Historical Review*, XXX (1951) 144–53.
    Some accounts prepared by an unknown executor of George Forrest (d. 1637).
288. MUNSLOW, F. W., 'Executorship Accounts in 1653', *Accountant*, CXL (1959) 218–19.
    The will and account book of Lyonell Tynley, lead-miner and merchant of Holmesfield, Derbyshire (d. 19 Nov. 1653).

S. FINANCIAL ACCOUNTING THEORY

289. AMERICAN TELEPHONE AND TELEGRAPH COMPANY, *Depreciation. History and Concepts in the Bell System* (1957) 154 pp.
    The depreciation experience of a large American public utility since 1884.
290. BOER, G., 'Replacement Cost: A Historical Look', *Accounting Review*, XLI (1966) 92–7.
    Replacement cost has received attention from theoreticians but practising accountants have largely ignored it.

SELECT BIBLIOGRAPHY

291. BRIEF, R. P., 'Nineteenth Century Accounting Error', *Journal of Accounting Research*, III (1965) 12-31.

    'Accounting error' is the failure to (*a*) systematically distinguish between capital and revenue expenditure, (*b*) periodically allocate the original cost of fixed assets to expense.

292. BRIEF, R. P., 'The Origin and Evolution of Nineteenth-Century Asset Accounting', *Business History Review*, XL (1966) 1-23.

    A study of the principles and practices of nineteenth-century asset accounting in the United Kingdom and the United States.

293. BRIEF, R. P., 'A Late Nineteenth Century Contribution to the Theory of Depreciation', *Journal of Accounting Research*, V (1967) 27-38.

    Reproduction of, and commentary on, O. G. Ladelle, 'The Calculation of Depreciation', *Accountant*, Nov. 1890.

294. CARSBERG, B. V., 'The Contribution of P. D. Leake to the Theory of Goodwill Valuation', *Journal of Accounting Research*, IV (1966) 1-15.

    Leake's work was 'a collection, a refinement, and, above all, a dissemination of the ideas which had been expressed by others'.

295. CHAMBERS, R. J., 'A Theory of the Development of Accounting Practices', pp. 341-63 of his *Accounting, Evaluation and Economic Behaviour* (Englewood Cliffs, N.J., Prentice-Hall, 1966).

    An attempt to explain why in accounting 'the tendency has been towards diffuseness of ideas and diversity of practices' (p. 359); see also his 'The Development of Accounting Theory', pp. 18-35 of CHAMBERS, R. J., GOLDBERG, L. and MATHEWS, R. L. (eds), *The Accounting Frontier* (Melbourne, Cheshire, 1965).

296. DEINZER, H. T., *Development of Accounting Thought* (New York, Holt, Rinehart & Winston, 1965) pp. 1-26.

    Three short chapters on the historical background to current controversies on accounting theory.

297. GOLDBERG, L., 'Concepts of Depreciation', *Accounting Review*, XXX (1955) 468-84; reprinted in GOLDBERG, L., *Concepts of Depreciation* (Sydney, Law Book Co., 1961) pp. 1-25, and in BAXTER, W. T., and DAVIDSON, S. (eds), *Studies in Accounting Theory* (London, Sweet & Maxwell, 2nd ed., 1962) pp. 236-58.

    The meanings and history of the word 'depreciation'.

298. KÄFER, K., 'A Brief Survey of Some Selected Theories of Accounts', pp. 6-38 of his *Theory of Accounts in Double-Entry Book-keeping* (Urbana, Ill., Center for International Education and Research in Accounting, Monograph 2, 1966).
Theories of double entry from Pacioli onwards.

299. LITHERLAND, D. A., 'Fixed Asset Replacement a Half Century Ago', *Accounting Review*, XXVI (1951) 475-80.
Some English views on fixed asset replacement and depreciation around 1900.

300. LITTLETON, A. C., 'Genealogy for Cost or Market', *Accounting Review*, XVI (1941) 161-7.
Convenience and expediency played the major rôle in the early appearances of the cost-or-market rule.

301. MASON, P., 'Illustrations of the Early Treatment of Depreciation', *Accounting Review*, VIII (1933) 209-18.
The examples range from Monteage's *Debtor and Creditor Made Easie* (1675) to the Annual Reports 1838-67 of the Boston and Worcester Railroad.

302. PARKER, R. H., 'Lower of Cost and Market in Britain and the United States: An Historical Survey', *Abacus*, I (1965) 156-72, reprinted in PARKER, R. H., and HARCOURT, G. C., *Readings in the Concept and Measurement of Income* (Cambridge University Press, 1969)
Lower of cost and market has survived because it embodies the rival concepts of historical cost and market value in a single rule.

303. PARKER, R. H., 'A Note on Savary's "Le Parfait Négociant"', *Journal of Accounting Research*, IV (1966) 260-1.
Savary recommended that merchandise which has not decreased in price should be valued at historical cost.

304. STOREY, R. K., *The Search for Accounting Principles* (New York, American Institute of Certified Public Accountants, 1964) 65 pp.
The historical background to the arguments about postulates and principles of the 1960's.

305. VANCE, L. L., 'Authority of History in Inventory Valuation', *Accounting Review*, XVIII (1943) 219-27.
A rejection of the Littleton thesis (see above) regarding the development of the cost-or-market rule.

306. ZEFF, S. A., 'Episodes in the Progression of Price-Level Accounting in the United States', *Accountants' Magazine*, LXVIII (1964) 285-304.

Developments since the 1930's in the United States in accounting for changing price levels.

T. EDUCATION

307. ALLEN, C. E., 'Growth of Accounting Instruction since 1900', *Accounting Review*, II (1927) 150–66.
  Traces the growth of instruction in accounting in American universities and colleges, 1900–26.
308. JACKSON, J. G. C., 'The History of Methods of Exposition of Double-Entry Book-keeping in England', § pp. 288–312.
  The ways in which the rules of debit and credit have been explained.
309. LOCKWOOD, J., 'Early University Education in Accountancy', *Accounting Review*, XIII (1938) 131–44.
  From the founding of the Wharton School of Finance and Commerce (1881) to the early days of the School of Commerce, Accounts and Finance (founded 1900) of New York University.
310. MENDES, H. E., 'The Development of Uniform Examinations', *Accounting Review*, XIX (1944) 139–42.
  The use of the American Institute of Accountants' examinations by state accountancy boards.
311. RICHARDSON, H. G., 'Business Training in Medieval Oxford', *American Historical Review*, XLVI (1941) 259–80.
  Thomas Sampson taught Latin, French, law and accounting at the University of Oxford in the fourteenth and early fifteenth centuries.
312. SAMPSON, R. J., 'American Accounting Education, Textbooks, and Public Practice Prior to 1900', *Business History Review*, XXXIV (1960) 459–66.
  A survey of the developments during the nineteenth century.
313. WILDMAN, J. R., 'Early Instruction in Accounting', *Accounting Review*, I (1926) 105–7.
  A personal reminiscence by an early student of accounting at New York University.
314. [ZEFF, S. A.], *The American Accounting Association: its first 50 years* (American Accounting Association, 1966) 96 pp.
  '... a compendious historical narrative of the progress of the American Accounting Association during its first fifty years'.

314(a). PICKARD, O. G., 'Office Work and Education 1848-1948', *Vocational Aspects*, I iii (1948) 221-43.
Includes a discussion of the teaching of book-keeping in Britain.

U. TERMINOLOGY

315. GOLDBERG, L., 'The Word "Stock"', *Australian Accountant*, XXVI (1956) 11-14.
The changing meaning of a word.
316. HATFIELD, H. R., 'The Early Use of "Capital"', *Quarterly Journal of Economics*, XLIX (1934) 162-3.
The final note of four on this subject: one by Cannan, XXXV (1921) 469-81; one by Richards, XL (1926) 329-38; and a previous one by Hatfield, XL (1926) 547-8.
317. YAMEY, B. S., 'The Word "Ledger"', *Accountancy*, LXXII (1961) 143.
An etymological note.

V. BIBLIOGRAPHIES, BIOGRAPHIES AND CHRONOLOGIES

318. [ABS, G., and others], 'Historical Dates in Accounting', *Accounting Review*, XXIX (1954) 486-93.
From taxation in Babylonia (4500 B.C.) to the revision and restatement of the American Institute of Accountants' *Accounting Research Bulletin* (1953).
319. BENTLEY, H. C., and LEONARD, R. S., *Bibliography of Works on Accounting by American Authors 1796-1934* (Boston, Harry C. Bentley, 1934-5), vol. 1 (1796-1900) 197 pp.; vol. 2 (1901-34) 408 pp.
The bibliography is both chronological and classified.
320. [CERBONI, G.], *Elenco cronologico delle opere di computisteria e ragioneria venute alle luce in Italia del 1202 sino al 1888* (Rome, Tipografia Nazionale di Reggiani e Soci, 4th ed., 1889) 280 pp.
Bibliography of accounting and arithmetic books published in Italy from Fibonacci's *Liber Abaci* (1202) to 1888.
321. EDWARDS, J. D., and SALMONSON, R. E. (compilers), *Contributions*

of *Four Accounting Pioneers - Kohler, Littleton, May, Paton* (East Lansing, Michigan State University, 1961) 238 pp.

Digests of the periodical writings of four influential accounting authors of the twentieth century.

322. GORDON, C., 'Books on Accountancy 1494-1600', *Transactions of the Bibliographical Society*, XIII (1913-15) 145-70.

Discusses the books of such authors as Pacioli, Manzoni, Ympyn, Oldcastle, Schweicker, Tagliente, Pietra and Mennher.

323. HAGERS, J., *Bouwstoffen voor de Geschiedenis van het boekhouden in de Nederlanden* (Rotterdam, G. Delwel & Co., 1903) 42 pp.

Bibliography of accounting books published in the Netherlands from 1543 (Ympyn) to 1901.

324. HATFIELD, H. R., and LITTLETON, A. C., 'A Check-List of Early Book-keeping Texts', *Accounting Review*, VII (1932) 194-206.

A bibliography of book-keeping textbooks published prior to 1850.

325. MILNE, K. L., 'Comparative Chronological Table', app. B (pp. 251-8) of his *The Accountant in Public Practice* (London, Butterworth, 1959).

The comparison is with the legal and medical professions.

326. REYMONDIN, G., *Bibliographie méthodique des Ouvrages en langue française parus de 1543 à 1908 sur la Science des Comptes* (Paris, Société Académique de Comptabilité, 1909) 330 pp.

Classification is by subject, but a chronological table of authors cited is also provided.

327. 'Steps in the Evolution of the Profession in the United Kingdom', *Accountant*, CXXXVII (1957) 544-5.

From the formation of the Society of Accountants in Edinburgh (31 Jan. 1853) to the integration of the Society of Incorporated Accountants within the three Chartered Institutes (2 Nov. 1957).

328. STEVELINCK, E., and HAULOTTE, R., *Galerie des Grands Auteurs Comptables* (Brussels, Éditions Comptabilité et Productivité).†

329. THOMSON, H. W., and YAMEY, B. S., 'Bibliography of Bookkeeping and Accounts - 1494 to 1650', *Accounting Research*, IX (1957) 239-57.

From Pacioli to Campaccio.

W. BANK ACCOUNTING

330. GOITEIN, S. D., 'Bankers' accounts from the eleventh century A.D.', *Journal of the Economic and Social History of the Orient*, IX (1966) 28–68.

    Bankers' accounts from the Fatimid period in Egypt.

331. HOLGATE, H. C. F., *English Bank Accounting and its Historical Background* (London, Staples Press, 1948) 148 pp.

    The factors that have influenced the development of bank accounting in England.

332. 'Mr Chest and Mr Box', *Westminster Bank Review*, Aug. 1952, pp. 14–17.§

    Eighteenth-century account books of a Derbyshire bank.

333. SHELTON, S. W., 'The Goldsmith Banker', *Three Banks Review*, no. 27 (1955) pp. 42–52.§

    Seventeenth-century ledgers of Child's Bank, London (absorbed in Glyn, Mills & Co. in 1924).

X. MISCELLANEOUS

334. BROWN, (Sister) I., *The Historical Development of the Use of Ratios in Financial Statement Analysis to 1933* (Washington, D.C., Catholic University of America Press, 1955) 28 pp.

    Mainly concerned with developments in the United States.

335. BRUNDAGE, P. F., 'Influence of Government Regulation on Development of Today's Accounting Practices', *Journal of Accountancy*, XC (1950) 384–91; reprinted in MURPHY, M. E. (ed.), *Selected Readings in Accounting and Auditing* (Englewood Cliffs, N.J., Prentice-Hall, 1952).

    A general account; refers to 'cost' and 'fair return' bases of regulatory bodies.

336. BRUNDAGE, P. F., 'Milestones on the Path of Accounting', *Harvard Business Review*, XXIX (1951) 71–81.

    Accounting and its environment in the United States in the first half of the twentieth century.

337. DE ROOVER, R., 'Early Accounting Problems of Foreign Exchange', *Accounting Review*, XIX (1944) 381–407.
Accounting for bills of exchange, with particular reference to early modern Italy.
338. FUSSELL, G. E. (ed.), *Robert Loder's Farm Accounts 1610–1620* (Camden 3rd ser., vol. LIII; London, Royal Historical Society, 1936). Introduction xxxi pp.; text, appendix, glossary and index 207 pp.
Combines 'primitive accounting form with evidence of keen understanding of economic calculation for business decision-making' (Yamey).
339. HAIN, H. P., 'Casting the Account', *Journal of Accounting Research* V (1967) 154–63.
The use of counting-boards by early accountants.
340. HAULOTTE, R., *De Luca Pacioli au Plan Comptable Général Belge (P.C.G.B.)* (Brussels, Éditions Comptabilité et Productivité, n.d.) 55 pp.
The development of charts of accounts and national accounting plans in Europe.
341. HILL, N. K., 'Accountancy Developments in a Public Utility Company in the Nineteenth Century', *Accounting Research*, VI (1955) 382–90.
The accounting history of the Imperial Continental Gas Association, 1824–1900, with a reproduction of the balance sheets of 31 Mar. 1926, and 31 Dec. 1900.
341(a). HORRIGAN, J. O., 'A Short History of Financial Ratio Analysis', *Accounting Review*, XLIII (1968) 284–94.
Concludes that the dominant approach has been 'pragmatical empiricism'.
342. JACOBSEN, L. E., 'The Ancient Inca Empire of Peru and the Double Entry Accounting Concept', *Journal of Accounting Research*, II (1964) 221–8.
The case for an Inca origin of double entry.
343. 'The Jubilee of *The Accountant*', *Accountant*, LXXI (1924) 497–501.
See also BACK, W. J., 'The First Half Century of "The Accountant"', *Economic Journal*, XXXV (1925) and BIRD, R., '*The Accountant*'s Seventy-Five Years', *Accountant*, CXXI (1949).

344. JUCIUS, M. J., 'Historical Development of Uniform Accounting', *Journal of Business*, XVI (1943) 219–29.

   Restricted to developments in the industrial field in the United States, 1875–c. 1932.

345. KEISTER, O. R., 'The Incan Quipu', *Accounting Review*, XXXIX (1964) 414–16.

   The quipu was a record-keeping device used by the Incas.

346. PARKER, R. H., 'Book-keeping and the African Slave Trade', *Accountants' Magazine*, LXII (1958) 116–19.

   Includes the accounts of a voyage made by the slave ship *La Fortuna* from Havana to West Africa and back in 1827.

347. PARKINSON, B. B., 'A Slaver's Accounts', *Accounting Research*, II (1951) 144–50.

   The triangular voyages; includes a voyage account of 1769.

348. PENNDORF, B., 'The Relation of Taxation to the History of the Balance Sheet', *Accounting Review*, V (1930) 243–51.

   The relation is traced for ancient Rome and for medieval Italy and Germany.

349. POLLINS, H., 'Aspects of Railway Accounting before 1868', § pp. 332–55.

   The problems of early railway accounting, with special reference to depreciation and the distinction between capital and revenue.

350. SILLÉN, O., 'Zur Geschichte der Betriebswirtschaftslehre in Schweden (ii)', *Zeitschrift für Handelswissenschaft und Handelspraxis*, vol. 4 (1929).†

   The literature on book-keeping in Sweden up to 1900.

351. STUDENSKI, P., *The Income of Nations* (New York, University Press, 1958) 554 pp.

   Includes material on the history of national income accounting.

352. 'The Woodhead Prize Account Ledger 1842–65', *Three Banks Review*, no. 76 (Dec. 1967) pp. 36–48.

   The ledger is mainly a record of money paid for the capture of vessels involved in illegal slave-trading.

353. YAMEY, B. S., 'Business Accounts', pp. 30–6 of BARKER, T. C., CAMPBELL, R. H., and MATHIAS, P., *Business History* (London, The Historical Association, 1960).

   Advice for business historians.

INDEX OF AUTHORS
To item numbers in the Bibliography

Abs, G., 318
Allen, C. E., 307
American Telephone and Telegraph Company, 289
Amodeo, D., 238
Anton, H. R., 269
Armet, H., 159
Arthur Andersen & Co., 202
Association of Certified and Corporate Accountants, 203
Aston, C. W., 239
Australian Society of Accountants, 204
Back, W. J., 343
Barton, A. D., 240
Batho, G. R., 94
Baxter, W. T., 185, 186, 187
Bentley, H. C., 319
Besta, F., 1
Bird, R., 343
Blagden, C., 121
Blanc, A., 86
Boer, G., 290
Boursy, A. V., 47
Boutell, W. S., 229, 281
Bowden, B. V., 282
Brief, R. P., 291, 292, 293
Broome, D. M., 162
Brown, (Sister) I., 334
Brown, R., 2
Brown, R. G., 48, 230
Bruchey, S. W., 188
Brulez, W., 69
Brummet, R. Lee, 241
Brundage, P. F., 335, 336
Burley, K. H., 122
Bursk, E. C., 3
Buttimer, H., 270
Carman, L. A., 70
Carsberg, B. V., 294
Casler, D. J., 205
Castellani, A., 49
Cerboni, G., 320

Chambers, R. J., 295
Chapin, N., 242
Chiaudano, M., 50
Chiera, E., 37
Claire, R. S., 271
Clark, D. T., 3
Cochrane, G., 231
Commonwealth Institute of Accountants, 206
Connell-Smith, G. E., 123
Coomber, R. R., 124, 146
Cooper, E., 207
Cooper Brothers & Co., 207
Cox, J. C., 95
Crivelli, P., 51
Crone, E., 71
Crossman, P., 243
Daniels, G. W., 125
de Cazaux, L. F. G., 244
Deinzer, H. T., 296
Delmouzou-Peppa, D., 38
Denholm-Young, N., 95(a)
Denucé, J., 72, 177
de Roover, F. E., 52, 53, 245
de Roover, R., 4, 55, 65, 70, 73, 75, 246, 337
de Waal, P. G. A., 76, 77
Dien, E. van, 208
Dijksterhuis, E. J., 71
Drew, J. A., 96
Dupont, A., 87
Duverger, E., 78
Edey, H. C., 158, 272, 273
Edwards, J. D., 209, 321
Edwards, R. S., 247, 248
Eldridge, H. J., 5
Fitzpatrick, R. J., 283
Forbes, R. J., 71
Forestié, E., 88
Foster, B. F., 6
Fowler, G. H., 97
Frankland, L., 5
Freeman, A. M., 174

Fryde, E. B., 126
Fujita, Y., 197
Fussell, G. E., 338
Garner, S. P., 249
Garrett, A. A., 210
Geijsbeek, J. B., 7
Gibson, S., 98
Gitti, V., 56
Goddard, R. H., 192
Goitein, S. D., 330
Goldberg, L., 127, 193, 297, 315
Gomberg, L., 8
Gonzalez Ferrando, J. M., 9
Gooder, E. A., 112
Gordon, C., 128, 146, 322
Grady, P., 211
Graham, A. W., 212
Gras, N. S. B. and E. C., 99
Green, W. L., 10
Gregory, R. H., 274
Grier, E., 39
Guigue, G., 90
Haerning, M., 213
Hagers, J., 323
Hain, H. P., 40, 339
Halcrow, E. M., 160
Hall, H., 161
Hart, A. T., 129
Hartsough, M. L., 184
Hasson, C. J., 130
Hatfield, H. R., 11, 316, 324
Haulotte, R., 12, 57, 180, 232, 328, 340
Have, O. Ten, 80, 81
Hawkins, D. F., 275
Hay, L. E., 286
Heath, P., 100
Heers, J., 58
Hein, L. W., 233, 250
Hidy, R. W., 3
Hill, N. K., 341
Hodgson, R. A., 131
Holgate, H. C. F., 331
Hone, N. J., 101
Horne, D. H., 132
Horrigan, J. O., 341(a)
Howard, S. E., 89, 189

Innes, C., 133
Institute of Chartered Accountants in England and Wales, 215
Institute of Chartered Accountants of Scotland, 214
Jack, S. M., 102
Jackson, J. G. C., 308
Jackson, J. H., 251
Jacobsen, L. E., 342
Jäger, E. L., 13, 14
James, M. E., 103
James, M. K., 145
Jeal, E. F., 216
Jenkinson, H., 162
Jennings, R. M., 190
Johnson, C., 163, 171
Johnston, K. S., 48
Jones, F. H., 276
Jones, T. B., 41
Jucius, M. J., 344
Käfer, K., 277, 298
Kats, P., 15, 59, 135, 136, 137, 138
Keister, O. R., 42, 43, 345
Kelly, J. P., 164
Kheil, C. P., 16, 60, 82
Kojima, O., 17
Kraayenhof, J., 217
Kulshrestha, H. S., 201
Kuperus, J. A., 79
Lamond, E., 104
Lane, F. C., 61, 62
Lapsley, C. T., 139
Latham, R. E., 105
Leonard, R. S., 319
Levett, A. E., 107
Lewis, N. B., 234
Litherland, D. A., 299
Littleton, A. C., 18, 19, 20, 21, 252, 300, 324
Livock, D. M., 165, 166
Lockwood, J., 309
Longfield, A. K., 175, 176
Lopez, R. S., 22
McRae, T. W., 284
McCredie, H., 194, 195, 196
McGrath, P., 140

SELECT BIBLIOGRAPHY

MacMillan, D. S., 196
Marple, R. P., 253
Maskell, R. E., 218
Mason, P., 301
Mattesich, R., 254
Melis, F., 23, 63
Mendes, H. E., 310
Merritt, B. D., 44
Meyer, P., 90
Mickwitz, G., 45
Millar, A. H., 141
Milne, K. L., 325
Minnaert, M. G. J., 71
Mollat, M., 91
Montgomerie, A., 287
Morrison, P. and E., 285
Most, K. S., 255
Moyer, C. A., 235
Munslow, F. W., 288
Murphy, M. E., 219, 220, 221, 222
Murray, D., 24
Myatt-Price, E. M., 108, 109, 110
Nielsen, D., 256
Nishikawa, K., 198
Normanton, E. L., 167
Noyce, G. E., 223
Oschinsky, D., 111
Page, F. M., 112
Pannekoek, A., 71
Parker, R. H., 224, 302, 303, 346
Parkinson, B. B., 347
Parsloe, G., 168
Peloubet, M. E., 25
Penndorf, B., 64, 178, 348
Peragallo, E., 26, 27
Pickard, O. G., 314(a)
Pickl, O., 179
Pollard, S., 142
Pollins, H., 236, 349
Poole, R. L., 169
Poynton, T. L., 225
Ramsay, G. B., 143
Ramsey, P., 144
Raymond, I. W., 22
Raymond, R. H., 257
Read, C., 113
Reymondin, G., 326

Richardson, H. G., 311
Rickert, E., 145
Robert, R., 170
Robinson, H. W., 226
Rogers, D. M., 258
Ste. Croix, G. E. M. de, 46
Salmonson, R. E., 321
Salzman, L. F., 114
Sampson, R. J., 312
Sapori, A., 65
Sarton, G., 83
Schneider, J., 92
Scorgie, M. B., 259
Shelton, S. W., 333
Shimme, S., 200
Sillén, O., 350
Simpson, A., 115
Sizer, J., 260
Slicher van Bath, B. H., 84
Smith, M., 260(a)
Smith, R. A. L., 116
Solomons, D., 28, 261
Stacey, N. A. H., 227
Staub, W. A., 237
Stenton, D. M., 171
Stephens, R. J., 262
Stevelinck, E., 57, 180, 328
Stone, E., 117
Storey, R. K., 304
Strickett, H. E., 278
Strieder, J., 181
Studenski, P., 351
Sutherland, P., 146
Tate, W. E., 118
Taylor, R. E., 66, 67
Theiss, E. L., 263
Thierfelder, H., 182
Thomson, H. W., 29, 158, 329
Tremel, L. F., 183
Tupling, G. H., 119
Vance, L. L., 305
Vanes, J., 147
Villers, R., 264
Vlaemminck, J.-H., 9, 30
Voke, A. J., 191
Volmer, J. G. Ch., 85
Wallace, E. G., 148

Wallace, E. L., 274
Weber, C., 266
Weber, K., 265
Weitnauer, A., 184
Wildman, J. R., 313
Wing, G. A., 267
Wolff, Ph., 93
Wolffe, B. P., 172
Wood-Legh, K. L., 120
Woolf, A. H., 31

Worthington, B., 228
Wren, M. C., 173
Wright, F. K., 268
Yamey, B. S., 20, 32, 33, 34, 35, 36, 143, 149, 150, 151, 152, 153, 154, 155, 156, 157, 158, 279, 317, 329, 353
Zeff, S. A., 306, 314
Zerbi, T., 68
Zimmerman, V. K., 21, 277

6 An Accounting Chronology

(1130 to 1966)[1]

IN this chapter an attempt has been made to set out the most important dates in the history of accounting since the twelfth century A.D., beginning with the accounting records of the English Crown (the first Pipe Roll, 1130–1) and the oldest surviving medieval business records (from Genoa, 1156–8). In adjoining columns there are given not only the political environment but also relevant events in the history of economic theory, law, taxation and management. Somewhat arbitrary decisions have sometimes had to be made between what is accounting and what is, say, economics or law.

Especially from the nineteenth century the emphasis is on the English-speaking world, but an effort has been made not to neglect other countries.

[1] I am grateful to Professor S. A. Zeff for comments on an earlier draft of this chapter. He is in no way responsible, however, for the final result.

Date	Accounting	Economic Theory, Law Taxation and Management	Political Environment
1130–1	First English Pipe Roll (during reign of Henry I).		
1135			Death of Henry I followed in England by civil war during reign of Stephen (d. 1154).
1152			Frederick I (Barbarossa) crowned Holy Roman Emperor.
1156–8	Oldest surviving medieval business records (from Genoa): those of the winding up of three successive temporary partnerships between Ingo da Volta (investing partner) and Ansaldo Baialardo (travelling partner).		
c. 1179	Dialogus de Scaccario (Dialogue of the Exchequer) by Richard son of Nigel, Treasurer of England: detailed practical treatise on government accounting.		
1188		Direct taxation of personal property in England introduced in the form of a crusading tax.	
1189–93			Third Crusade.
13th C.	Walter of Henley's Husbandry describes 'charge and discharge' accounting. Genoese ship-accounts show evidence of depreciation.		

AN ACCOUNTING CHRONOLOGY   129

Date	Accounting	Economic Theory, Law Taxation and Management	Political Environment
1202	*Liber Abaci* of Leonardo Fibonacci of Pisa includes discussions of book-keeping and compound interest, and stresses the superiority of arabic over roman numerals.		
1202–4			Fourth Crusade.
1211	Oldest surviving example of medieval book-keeping: account book of an unknown Florentine banking partnership.		
1215			Magna Carta sealed.
1296–1305	Account book of Rinieri Fini and brothers of Florence; in paragraph form, probably in double entry.		
1299–1300	Ledger of the Farolfi Company of Florence; perhaps in double entry. Includes an example of prepaid rent.		
14th C.		Inns of Courts established in England.	
1303			*Carta mercatoria* of Edward I grants privileges to foreign merchants in England.
1304–7	Oldest surviving account book from South Germany – that of the Holzschuhers, a family partnership of Nuremberg drapers.		

Date	Accounting	Economic Theory, Law Taxation and Management	Political Environment
1305–8	Cash book of London branch of Gallerani Company of Siena; perhaps in double entry.		
1316	Earliest reference to accountants and auditors in Ireland.		
1318–22	Cost accounting by Francesco del Bene & Co., wool-manufacturers of Florence.		
1320–3	Oldest surviving French account book – that of an unknown draper of Lyons (not in double entry).		
1329–60	Earliest surviving Hanseatic account book – that of Hermann and Johann Wittenborg.		
1337–1453			Hundred Years' War between England and France.
1340	Oldest surviving accounts definitely kept in double entry – those of the *massari* (stewards) of Genoa.	First European paper mill set up at Fabriano in Italy.	
1347–51			Black Death devastates Europe.
c. 1390	From this date accounts of Francesco di Marco Datini, merchant of Prato, kept in double entry; show evidence of job cost accounting, accrual accounting and depreciation.		

AN ACCOUNTING CHRONOLOGY 131

Date	Accounting	Economic Theory, Law Taxation and Management	Political Environment
15th & 16th C.	Medici industrial partnerships used cost-accounting techniques.		
1422	Accounts of the mint at Ragusa show evidence of cost accounting.		
1436–9	Ledger of Borromeo Company of London.		
1453			Capture of Constantinople by Ottoman Turks.
1455–85			Wars of the Roses in England.
1458	Bendetto Cotrugli, *Della Mercatura et del mercante* (Ragusa), describes double entry (not printed until 1573).		
1492			First expedition of Columbus.
1492–1503	Ledger of Andrew Halyburton (Scotland) – not in double entry.		
1494	Luca Pacioli, *Summa de Aritmética, Geometria Proportioni et Proportionalità* (Venice) – first printed book to include description of double-entry bookkeeping.		Charles VIII of France invades Italy and expels Medicis from Florence (restored by Imperial troops 1530).
1497			Vasco da Gama reaches India via Cape of Good Hope.
c. 1500	Up to this date, double entry a		

Date	Accounting	Economic Theory, Law Taxation and Management	Political Environment
	business technique known only to Italian merchants.		
1517			Martin Luther's 95 Theses.
1518	H. Schreiber (Grammateus), *Ayn new küntslich Buech* (Nuremberg) – first German work on book-keeping (does not discuss double entry). Matthäus Schwarz's manuscript on book-keeping (including double entry).		
1520	Earliest reference to merchants' account books in Japan.		
1522–7	Ledger of Thomas Howell – oldest surviving English ledger kept in double entry (written up in Spain).		
1531–4	The accounts of Raffaello di Francesco de' Medici, cloth-manufacturers of Florence: early example of cost accounting.		
1534	D. Manzoni, *Quaderno doppio col suo giornale* ... (Venice).		Act of Supremacy severes English Church from Rome.
1536–9			Dissolution of the monasteries in England.
1542		Earliest English bankruptcy statute.	
1543	Jan Ympyn's *Niewe Instructie* ... and *Nouvelle Instruction*		

AN ACCOUNTING CHRONOLOGY 133

Date	Accounting	Economic Theory, Law Taxation and Management	Political Environment
	... (both published in Antwerp – earliest books on double entry in Flemish and French.) Hugh Oldcastle, *A profitable treatyce* ... (London): first book on double entry in English (no surviving copy).		
1543–63			Council of Trent (Catholic Reformation)
1547	*A Notable and very excellente woorke* ... (London) – English translation of Ympyn's book.		Death of Henry VIII of England.
1549	W. Schweicker, *Zwifach Buchhalten* (Nuremberg) – first German book on double entry.		
1550	V. Mennher de Kempten, *Practique brifue pour cyfrer et tenir livres de compte* ... (Antwerp).		
1553	James Peele, *The maner and fourme how to kepe a perfecte reconyng* ... (London) – the earliest printed book-keeping text of purely English origin.		Mary I becomes Queen of England.
1558		Jean Trenchant, *L'Aritmétique departie en troys livres* (Lyons) – first book to include compound-interest tables.	French capture Calais, last English possession in France. Elizabeth I becomes Queen of England.

134 MANAGEMENT ACCOUNTING

Date	Accounting	Economic Theory, Law Taxation and Management	Political Environment
1563–7	The accounts (kept in Italian) of Christopher Plantin, printer and publisher of Antwerp: early example of cost accounting.		
1565	A. Rocha, *Compendio y breve instruction por tener libros* (Barcelona) – first book in Spanish on double entry (translation of Mennher's book of 1550).		St Augustine, first settlement in what is now the United States, founded by Spain.
1581	Collegio dei Raxonati (association of accountants) founded in Venice.		
1582		Simon Stevin, *Tables of Interest* (Antwerp) stated net-present-value criterion for choosing between alternative investments.	
1585			Antwerp, sacked by Spaniards, loses its importance in international trade to Amsterdam.
1588	John Mellis, *A Briefe instruction* . . . (London): oldest surviving book in English on double entry.		Defeat of Spanish Armada by English.
1598			Edict of Nantes grants toleration to Huguenots; end of French religious wars.
1600		First endorsed bill of exchange (Naples).	

AN ACCOUNTING CHRONOLOGY 135

Date	Accounting	Economic Theory, Law Taxation and Management	Political Environment
1604	Simon Stevin, *Vorsteliche bouckhouding op de Italiaansche wijse* ... (Leyden) (published in French in 1608 as *Livre de Compte de Prince à la manière d'Italie* ...).		
1610		Dutch East India Company introduces the term 'share'.	
1610–20	Robert Loder's farm accounts: primitive in accounting form, but show evidence of understanding of economic calculation for decision-making.		
1603–1867			Tokugawa Shogunate in Japan.
1615	Earliest surviving Japanese account books.		
1618–48			Thirty Years War.
1620			Sailing of *Mayflower*.
1621		First Scottish Act relating to bankruptcy.	
1624			Foundation of New Amsterdam (renamed New York 1664).
1635	Richard Dafforne, *The Merchants Mirrour* ... (London).		
1642			Death of Richelieu; succeeded by Mazarin. New Zealand and Tasmania discovered by Tasman.
1642–4		Blaise Pascal, French philosopher and	

Date	Accounting	Economic Theory, Law Taxation and Management	Political Environment
		mathematician, makes the first mechanical calculating-machine.	
1643			Death of Louis XIII of France; accession of Louis XIV.
1645–1723	George Watson of Edinburgh, first Scottish professional accountant.		
1673		French Ordinance *Pour le Commerce* (Code Savary).	
1675		Jacques Savary, *Le Parfait Négociant* (Paris) includes discussion of inventory valuation.	
1683	R. Colinson, *Idea Rationaria* ... (Edinburgh) – first book on double entry published in Scotland.		
1685			Revocation of Edict of Nantes by Louis XIV. Death of Charles II.
1688			'Glorious Revolution' in England.
1694		Bank of England founded.	
1696	S. Ammonet, *The Key of knowledge* ... (Dublin) – first work on book-keeping published in Ireland.		
1697	John Collins, *The Perfect Method of Merchants Accompts* (London) – contains material on factory accounting.		

AN ACCOUNTING CHRONOLOGY 137

Date	Accounting	Economic Theory, Law Taxation and Management	Political Environment
1707			Act of Union (England and Scotland).
1720		South Sea Bubble. 'Bubble Act.'	
1720–1	Charles Snell's 'Observations Made upon Examining the Books of Sawbridge and Company'.		
1729		Attorneys' and Solicitors' Act formalised the system of training based on apprenticeship (5-year articles), later copied by the accounting profession in Britain.	
1750	James Dodson, *The Accountant* (London), describes batch costing.		
1756		James Dodson's unpublished 'First Lecture on Insurances' laid down principles of life assurance for first time.	
1756–63			Seven Years War (known in U.S.A. as French and Indian War), at end of which Britain, not France, dominant in North America and India.
1758		François Quesnay, *Tableau Économique*, displays diagrammatically the interdependence of the different economic classes and sectors and	

138 MANAGEMENT ACCOUNTING

Date	Accounting	Economic Theory, Law Taxation and Management	Political Environment
1771		the flow of payments between them. Richard Price, *Observations on Reversionary Payments*, helps to lay the foundations of a scientific system of life assurance. Arkwright founds first spinning-mill in England.	
1776	Earliest mention of a professional accountant in London.	Adam Smith, *An Inquiry into the Nature and Causes of the Wealth of Nations* – the foundation of classical political economy.	American Declaration of Independence.
1777	Wardhaugh Thompson, *The Accountant's Oracle* (York), describes process costing.		
1783			Peace of Versailles ends American War of Independence.
1787			United States Constitution signed.
1788	Robert Hamilton, *Introduction to Merchandise* (Edinburgh): leading British text on book-keeping.		Colonisation of Australia begins.
1789			French Revolution begins. George Washington first President of U.S.A.
1793			Execution of Louis XVI of France.
1795	Edmond Dégrange (père), *La tenue des livres rendue facile* ... (Paris): important		

Date	Accounting	Economic Theory, Law Taxation and Management	Political Environment
	French text on book-keeping.		
1796	Edward Jones, *English System of Book-keeping* ... (Bristol) – an unsuccessful attack on double entry.		
1798		T. R. Malthus, *An Essay on the Principle of Population*.	
1799		Income tax introduced in Britain by William Pitt the younger (repealed 1802).	Napoleon Bonaparte First Consul of France.
1803		Addington's Income Tax Act lays the basis of the British system of taxation at source and schedular assessment.	U.S.A. purchases Louisiana from France.
1805			Battles of Trafalgar and Austerlitz.
1807		French commercial law code.	
1810	Charles Thomas of Colmar, Alsace, makes the first commercially successful calculating-machine.		
1812–14			War between U.S.A. and Great Britain.
1815			Battle of Waterloo. End of French Revolutionary and Napoleonic Wars.
1816		Income tax lapses in Britain (until 1842).	
1817	Anselme Payen, *Essai sur la Tenue des Livres d'un Manufac-*	David Ricardo, *Principles of Political Economy and Taxation*:	

Date	Accounting	Economic Theory, Law Taxation and Management	Political Environment
	turier (Paris): first important French work on cost accounting.	most important work in the tradition of classical economics.	
1818	F. W. Cronhelm, *Double Entry by Single* (London), explains double entry algebraically; probably first text to discuss a perpetual inventory.		
1819			U.S.A. obtains Florida from Spain.
1821		Period of articles for solicitors' articled clerk in England reduced from five years to three for a graduate.	
1823		Law Society founded. Charles Babbage begins construction of a 'difference engine'.	Monroe Doctrine proclaimed.
1825	L. F. G. de Cazaux, *De la Comptabilité dans une Entreprise Industrielle . . .* (Toulouse) – discusses business budgets.	Repeal of the 'Bubble Act' of 1720.	
1826	Tallies used for the last time in British governmental accounting.		
1830			Liverpool–Manchester railway completed. Beginning of the 'railway age'.
1831		English Bankruptcy Act creates an independent court of	

Date	Accounting	Economic Theory, Law Taxation and Management	Political Environment
		bankruptcy and official assignees.	
1832		Charles Babbage, *On the Economy of Machinery and Manufacturers* (London).	1st Reform Bill passed in Britain.
1834		Babbage invents principle of the 'analytical engine'.	Abolition of slavery in British Empire.
1836–7		Written examinations introduced for English attorneys and solicitors.	
1837		Isaac Pitman invents shorthand.	Victoria becomes Queen of Britain
1838		A. Cournot, *Researches into the Mathematical Principles of the Theory of Wealth*: forerunner of marginalist and mathematical economics.	
1841			New Zealand proclaimed British colony.
1842		Peel revives income tax in Britain.	
1843		Earliest known set of bond tables published by Joseph M. Price in New York. *The Economist* first published.	
1844		U.K. Joint Stock Companies Act made possible incorporation (but not limited liability) by registration.	

142 MANAGEMENT ACCOUNTING

Date	Accounting	Economic Theory, Law Taxation and Management	Political Environment
1848		Institute of Actuaries formed in England. J. S. Mill, *Principles of Political Economy* (London).	'Year of Revolutions' in Europe. *Communist Manifesto*.
1850		D. Lardner, *Railway Economy* (London) – clearly distinguishes between fixed and variable costs.	
1852		Council of Legal Education set up by the Inns of Court for 'maintenance of a uniform system for the legal education of students before admission to the Bar'.	Second Empire proclaimed in France.
1853–4	Society of Accountants in Edinburgh founded and given royal charter: first of the modern professional accountancy bodies.		
1853–5	Institute of Accountants and Actuaries in Glasgow formed and given royal charter.		
1854–6			Crimean War.
1855		U.K. Companies Act makes possible limited liability by registration.	
1856	Scottish Bankruptcy Act provides much work for accountants (anticipates English Act of 1869).	Faculty of Actuaries formed in Scotland.	
1857–8			Indian Mutiny.

AN ACCOUNTING CHRONOLOGY 143

Date	Accounting	Economic Theory, Law Taxation and Management	Political Environment
1861	English Bankruptcy Act expressly mentions accountants as eligible for appointment as official assignees.		Abraham Lincoln becomes President of U.S.A.
1861–5			American Civil War.
1862	U.K. Companies Act creates position of official liquidator thus encouraging growth of accounting profession.	U.K. Companies Act: a consolidating Act; the principal Act until 1908.	
1865			Assassination of Abraham Lincoln. 13th Amendment to U.S. Constitution abolishes slavery.
1866		Overend & Gurney failure.	
1867	Society of Accountants in Aberdeen receives charter.	Karl Marx, *Das Kapital*, vol. 1.	Canada becomes a Dominion. U.S.A. purchases Alaska from Russia.
1868			Meiji restoration in Japan.
1869	English Bankruptcy Act by substituting trustees for official assignees provides much work for accountants.		Suez Canal opened.
1870	Incorporated Society of Liverpool Accountants and Institute of Accountants in London founded.		
1870–1			Franco-Prussian War.
1871	Manchester Institute of Accountants established.	W. S. Jevons, *Theory of Political Economy* (London) – 'In com-	William I of Prussia becomes German Emperor.

144 MANAGEMENT ACCOUNTING

Date	Accounting	Economic Theory, Law Taxation and Management	Political Environment
		merce, bygones are for ever bygones.'	Third Republic in France.
1872	G. Cerboni, *Primi saggi di logismografia* (Rome): very influential in Europe.	Compulsory examinations for admission to English Bar.	
1873		First successful typewriter (designed by C. L. Scholes, produced by Remington).	
1874	*The Accountant* (London) first published.		
1874–7		Leon Walras, *Eléments d'Économie politique pure*.	
1875		*Ashbury Railway Co. v. Riche* – enunciation of doctrine of *ultra vires*.	
1876		Concept of opportunity cost formulated by Friedrich von Wieser (in a paper not published until 1929).	
1877	Sheffield Institute of Accountants established.		
1878	Thomas Battersby, *The Perfect Double Entry Book-keeper* (Manchester) – describes contemporary cost accounting.	Failure of the City of Glasgow Bank. First cash register.	
1879	U.K. Companies Act introduces compulsory annual audit for all banking companies registered thereafter with limited liability.		

AN ACCOUNTING CHRONOLOGY 145

Date	Accounting	Economic Theory, Law Taxation and Management	Political Environment
1880	Institute of Chartered Accountants in England and Wales formed by amalgamation of Liverpool, London, Manchester and Sheffield institutes. Association of Accountants in Montreal incorporated.		
1881	F. W. Pixley, *Auditors, Their Duties and Responsibilities* (London) – first important text on auditing.	Wharton School of Finance and Commerce established at University of Pennsylvania: first American collegiate school of business.	
1883	English Bankruptcy Act by providing for appointment of Official Receivers deprived accountants of much of their business. Institute of Chartered Accountants of Ontario incorporated.		
1884	Ewing Matheson, *The Depreciation of Factories* (London).		
1885	Society of Incorporated Accountants and Auditors (amalgamated with U.K. Chartered Institutes, 1957) and Corporate Treasurers' and Accountants' Institute (renamed Institute of Municipal Treasurers	Karl Marx, *Das Kapital*, vol. 2.	Death of General Gordon at Khartoum.

Date	Accounting	Economic Theory, Law Taxation and Management	Political Environment
	and Accountants, 1901; received roya charter 1959) established in U.K. Henry Metcalfe, *The Cost of Manufactures* (New York). William Burrough's adding-machine. Adelaide Society of Accountants formed (earliest antecedent body of Institute of Chartered Accountants in Australia).		
1886	Incorporated Institute of Accountants of Victoria formed (oldest antecedent body of Australian Society of Accountants).		
1887	E. Garcke and J. M. Fells, *Factory Accounts* (London) – 1st edition of earliest important English textbook on cost accounting.	A. M. Wellington, *The Economic Theory of the Location of Railways* (New York) 2nd ed., shows understanding of differential costs and revenues. Leeds Estate Building & Investment Society Ltd v. Shepherd – first important English case on auditing.	
1888	Institute of Chartered Accountants in Ireland received charter.	London *Financial Times* first issued.	
1889	*Incorporated Accountants Journal* first published (renamed *Accountancy*, 1938). G. P. Norton, *Textile Manufacturers' Book-keeping*.	F. von Wieser, *Der Natürliche Wert*. Lee v. Neuchatel Asphalte Co. Ltd – first important English case on divisible profits.	Suez Canal internationalised and neutralised.

Date	Accounting	Economic Theory, Law Taxation and Management	Political Environment
1890		1st ed. of Alfred Marshall, *Principles of Economics*. Failure of Baring's Bank, London. Hollerith punched cards used to analyse U.S. census returns. Royal Economic Society formed in U.K. U.K. Partnership Act.	
1892	1st ed. of L. R. Dicksee, *Auditing* (London) (17th ed. published in 1951).		Panama scandal in France.
1893–4		Concept of opportunity cost published by American economists Green and Davenport.	
1894	Incorporated Institute of Accountants of New Zealand formed.	Death duties introduced in Britain.	Dreyfus case in France.
1895		Income tax declared unconstitutional in U.S.A. Karl Marx, *Das Kapital*, vol. 3. London School of Economics and Political Science founded.	
1895–6		*London and General Bank* and *Kingston Cotton Mill* cases on duties and liabilities of auditors.	
1896	*Financial Circular* first published (renamed *Local Government Finance*, 1935).		

Date	Accounting	Economic Theory, Law Taxation and Management	Political Environment
	J. Slater Lewis, *The Commercial Organisation of Factories* (London). First C.P.A. Law in U.S.A. (New York State).		
1897	*Accountants' Magazine* first published. First State Society of Certified Public Accountants established in New York.		
1898			Spanish-American War.
1899		J. B. Clark, *The Distribution of Wealth* – first major American book on economics.	
1899–1902			Boer War.
1900	U.K. Companies Act makes annual audit obligatory for all registered companies.	U.K. Companies Act distinguishes between public and private companies.	British Labour Party founded.
1901	Corporate Treasurers' and Accountants' Institute incorporated as The Institute of Municipal Treasurers and Accountants. Alexander Hamilton Church, 'The Proper Distribution of Establishment Charges', published in *Engineering Magazine* (vols XXI–XXII) (reprinted in book form, 1916), advocates use of production centres.		Death of Queen Victoria. Assassination of President McKinley. Commonwealth of Australia comes into being.

Date	Accounting	Economic Theory, Law Taxation and Management	Political Environment
1902	Birmingham University establishes first chair of accounting in U.K. United States Steel Co. issues a consolidated balance sheet.		
1903	Henry Hess, 'Manufacturing: Capital, Costs and Profits', *Engineering Magazine*, vol. XXVI – first article on the break-even chart. Institute of Chartered Accountants in South Africa formed. U.K. Finance Act defines an 'accountant' as a 'person who has been admitted as a member of an incorporated society of accountants' and precipitates an outburst of new accounting bodies.	F. W. Taylor, 'Shop Management', *Transactions of the American Society of Mechanical Engineers* (Paper 1003, vol. XXIV): includes reference to management by exception.	
1904	Henry Rand Hatfield becomes first holder of a full-time accounting professorship at a U.S. university (California at Berkeley). First international congress of accountants held at St Louis, Missouri.		*Entente cordiale* between France and Britain.
1904–5			Russo-Japanese War.
1905	*Journal of Accountancy* and *Certified*		Abortive revolution in Russia.

Date	Accounting	Economic Theory, Law Taxation and Management	Political Environment
	Accountants Journal (entitled *Accountants Journal* 1946–66) first published. Morrell W. Gaines, 'Tabulating-Machine Cost-Accounting for Factories of Diversified Product', *Engineering Magazine*, vol. xxx.		
1906		Irving Fisher, *The Nature of Capital and Income* (New York).	
1907	U.S. Treasury changes from single- to double-entry book-keeping. U.S. Interstate Commerce Commission specifies a uniform system of accounts for railroads (beginning of regulatory accounting).	Irving Fisher, *The Rate of Interest* (New York).	
1908	U.K. Companies Act makes publication of balance sheets compulsory for public companies. C. E. Sprague, *The Philosophy of Accounts* (New York). W. M. Cole, *Accounts – Their Construction and Interpretation* (Boston). John Whitmore, 'Shoe Factory Cost Accounts', *Journal of Accountancy* (vol. vi) – first description of a standard costing system.	Harvard Graduate School of Business Administration started.	Austria annexes Bosnia and Herzegovina.

AN ACCOUNTING CHRONOLOGY 151

Date	Accounting	Economic Theory, Law Taxation and Management	Political Environment
1909	Harrington Emerson, *Efficiency as a Basis for Operation and Wages* (New York) emphasises standard costing. H. R. Hatfield, *Modern Accounting* (New York). Fabio Besta, *La Ragioneria* (Milan) 1st ed. J. Lee Nicholson, *Factory Organization and Costs* (New York).		
1910	H. L. Gantt, *Work, Wages and Profits* (New York).		Union of South Africa becomes a dominion.
1911	*Canadian Chartered Accountant* first published.	F. W. Taylor, *The Principles of Scientific Management* (New York). F. B. Gilbreth, *Motion Study* (New York).	Revolution in Mexico.
1912	R. H. Montgomery, *Auditing Theory and Practice* (New York) – 1st ed. of first important American text on auditing.		Proclamation of Chinese Republic. First Balkan War.
1913		Federal income tax introduced in U.S.A.	Second and Third Balkan Wars.
1914	1st ed. of F. R. M. de Paula, *Principles of Auditing* (London). E. T. Elbourne, *Factory Administration and Accounts* (London) – influential British text which helped to spread costing techniques during First World War.		First World War begins. Opening of Panama Canal.

Date	Accounting	Economic Theory, Law Taxation and Management	Political Environment
1914–18	During the First World War in U.K. income tax replaces bankruptcy as second branch, after auditing, of most accountants' professional work.	During the First World War standard rate of income tax in U.K. rises from 1s 2d to 6s. The law is consolidated in the Income Tax Act, 1918.	
1916	American Association of Public Accountants changed its name to American Institute of Accountants. American Association of University Instructors in Accounting formed.	Henri Fayol, *Administration Industrielle et Générale* (Paris). U.S. Supreme Court rules income-tax law is constitutional.	Easter Rebellion in Dublin.
1917	*Approved Methods for Preparation of Balance Sheet Statements* published by American Institute of Accountants and Federal Reserve Board.		Russian Revolution. U.S.A. enters First World War.
1918			End of First World War.
1918–19	G. Charter Harrison, 'Cost Accounting to Aid Production' published in *Industrial Management* (in book form, 1921).		
1919	Institute of Cost and Works Accountants established in U.K.; National Association of Cost Accountants formed in U.S.A. (name changed to National	Institute of Industrial Administration formed in U.K. (absorbed by British Institute of Management, 1951).	Treaty of Versailles.

AN ACCOUNTING CHRONOLOGY 153

Date	Accounting	Economic Theory, Law Taxation and Management	Political Environment
	Association of Accountants, 1957). Chair of accounting established at University of Edinburgh (first in Scotland).		
1920	*Accountants' Index* first published.	C. E. Knoeppel, *Graphic Production Control* (New York).	League of Nations established (not joined by U.S.A.). Prohibition comes into force in U.S.A.
1921	American Society of Certified Public Accountants founded. *Cost Accountant* first published (renamed *Management Accounting*, 1965). U.S. General Accounting Office established.		
1922	W. A. Paton, *Accounting Theory* (New York). *Harvard Business Review* first published. J. O. McKinsey, *Budgetary Control* (New York) – first comprehensive work on business budgeting. *Accountants' Journal* (N.Z.) first published.		Washington Naval Agreement between U.S.A., Britain and Japan. Irish Rebellion; Irish Free State officially proclaimed. Mussolini marches on Rome and forms Fascist government.
1923	1st ed. of *Accountants' Handbook*.	J. M. Clark, *Studies in the Economics of Overhead Costs* (Chicago) – first close look at cost accounting by an economist.	Union of Soviet Socialist Republics established.

154 MANAGEMENT ACCOUNTING

Date	Accounting	Economic Theory, Law Taxation and Management	Political Environment
1924	J. O. McKinsey, *Managerial Accounting* (Chicago).		First Labour government in Britain. Death of Lenin and Woodrow Wilson.
1925	*N.A.C.A. Bulletin* first published (name changed to *N.A.A. Bulletin* 1957, to *Management Accounting* 1965).		Locarno Conference and Treaties.
1926	*Accounting Review* and *Cost and Management* first published.		General Strike in Britain. Germany joins League of Nations.
1927	H. R. Hatfield, *Accounting* (New York).		Financial crisis in Germany.
1928	Institute of Chartered Accountants in Australia incorporated.	*Journal of Business* (of University of Chicago) first published.	Kellogg–Briand Pact 'outlawing war'.
1929	J. B. Canning, *Economics of Accountancy* (New York).	U.K. Companies Act.	Wall Street Crash. Beginning of Great Depression.
1930	U.K. government committee recommends against registration of accountants. *Chartered Accountant in Australia* first published.	E. L. Grant, *Principles of Engineering Economy*, 1st ed.	
1931	*Ultramares Corporation v. Touche Niven & Co.* Controllers Institute of America formed (renamed Financial Executives' Institute 1963).		Britain abandons the gold standard. Statute of Westminster defines Dominion status.
1932	Report of the American Institute's Special Committee on		F. D. Roosevelt elected president of U.S.A.

AN ACCOUNTING CHRONOLOGY

Date	Accounting	Economic Theory, Law Taxation and Management	Political Environment
	Cooperation with Stock Exchanges. Royal Mail case in U.K. leads to criticism of secret reserves. *Controller* first published (renamed *Financial Executive*, 1962).		U.S. Index of common stock prices reaches its lowest point.
1933	C. E. Knoeppel, *Profit Engineering* (New York). A. C. Littleton, *Accounting Evolution to 1900* (New York).	U.S. Securities Act. Joan Robinson, *The Economics of Imperfect Competition*, and E. Chamberlin, *The Theory of Monopolistic Competition*. A. A. Berle Jr and G. C. Means, *The Modern Corporation and Private Property* (New York) discusses the separation of ownership and control.	21st Amendment to U.S. Constitution repeals Prohibition. Hitler becomes German Chancellor. 'New Deal' begins in U.S.A. U.S.A. and Canada abandon the gold standard.
1933–4	New York Stock Exchange requires that all listed corporations should have an audit certificate from an independent certified public accountant.		
1934		U.S. Securities Exchange Act; Securities and Exchange Commission formed.	Purge of Russian Communist Party begins. Attempted Nazi coup in Austria; murder of Dollfuss.
1935			Saar reincorporated in Germany after plebiscite.

Date	Accounting	Economic Theory, Law Taxation and Management	Political Environment
1935–6	American Association of University Instructors in Accounting reconstituted as the American Accounting Association.		Italo-Abyssinian War.
1936	Merger of American Institute of Accountants and American Society of Certified Public Accountants. H. W. Sweeney, *Stabilized Accounting* (New York). American Accounting Association, *Tentative Statement of Accounting Principles affecting Corporate Reports.* Jonathan N. Harris, 'What Did We Earn Last Month?', *N.A.(C.)A. Bulletin:* first important article on direct costing. *Australian Accountant* first published.	J. M. Keynes, *General Theory of Employment, Interest and Money* (London).	Germany occupies demilitarised zone of the Rhineland. Abdication of Edward VIII.
1936–9			Spanish Civil War.
1937	U.S. Securities and Exchange Commission issues its first Accounting Series Release.	Profits tax on companies introduced in U.K. (called 'national defence contribution' until 1946; abolished by 1965 Finance Act).	
1938	T. H. Sanders, H. R. Hatfield, and U. Moore, *A Statement of Accounting Principles* published by	Chester Barnard, *The Functions of the Executive* (Harvard University Press).	Germany annexes Austria. Munich Crisis.

Date	Accounting	Economic Theory, Law Taxation and Management	Political Environment
	American Institute of Accountants. Candidates for C.P.A. certificate in New York State required to be college graduates.		
1939	Following the McKesson & Robbins case physical verification of inventory quantities and direct confirmation of accounts receivable become part of generally accepted standards of auditing procedure in the United States. American Institute of Accountants begins publication of Accounting Research Bulletins and Statements on Auditing Procedures. Association of Certified and Corporate Accountants formed in U.K. by absorption of Corporation of Accountants by London Association of Accountants. S. Gilman, *Accounting Concepts of Profit* (New York). U.S. Revenue Act permits use of LIFO method of inventory costing.	F. J. Roethlisberger and W. J. Dickson, *Management and the Worker* (Harvard University Press) – report on the Hawthorne experiments.	Dismemberment of Czechoslovakia. German invasion of Poland begins Second World War.
1939–45		During the Second World War the	

158 MANAGEMENT ACCOUNTING

Date	Accounting	Economic Theory, Law Taxation and Management	Political Environment
		standard rate of income tax in the U.K. rises from 5s 6d to 10s. The 'pay as you earn' system of taxing salaries begins in 1944. Operational research developed for military purposes in U.K. and U.S.A.	
1940	Institute of Internal Auditors formed. U.S. Securities and Exchange Commission issues Regulation S-X. W. A. Paton and A. C. Littleton, *An Introduction to Corporate Accounting Standards* published by American Accounting Association.		Winston Churchill becomes British Prime Minister. Fall of France. Battle of Britain.
1941		W. W. Leontief, *The Structure of the American Economy, 1919–1929* (Harvard University Press) – the classic work on input–output analysis.	Germany invades Russia. Pearl Harbor; U.S.A. enters Second World War.
1942	First Recommendation on Accounting Principles issued by Institute of Chartered Accountants in England and Wales.	Magnetic tape invented.	Fall of Singapore. Battle of El Alamein.
1943	G. O. May, *Financial Accounting* (New York) – a 'distillation of experience' of a leading practitioner.	L. Urwick, *The Elements of Administration* (New York) – concise statement of classical organisation theory.	Russian victory at Stalingrad. Unconditional surrender of Italy.

AN ACCOUNTING CHRONOLOGY 159

Date	Accounting	Economic Theory, Law Taxation and Management	Political Environment
1944	*Internal Auditor* first published. 1st ed. of *Accountants' Cost Handbook*.	J. von Neumann and O. Morgenstern, *Theory of Games and Economic Behaviour* (Princeton University Press). First automatic computer (A.S.C.C.).	'D-Day' landings in Normandy.
1945		Elton Mayo, *The Social Problems of an Industrial Civilisation* (Harvard U.P.) H. A. Simon, *Administrative Behaviour* (New York) 1st ed.	Deaths of Roosevelt, Hitler and Mussolini. Dropping of atomic bomb. End of Second World War. Attlee forms Labour government in Britain. United Nations Organisation comes into formal existence.
1946	*Journal of Finance* first published.	First electronic computer (ENIAC).	Nuremberg Trials.
1947	All U.S. labour unions required to prepare financial statements.	Simplex method of linear programming developed by G. B. Dantzig. British Institute of Management founded.	Truman Doctrine. Marshall Aid. Taft-Hartley Act passed by U.S. Congress. India and Pakistan become independent.
1948	U.K. Companies Act – 'group accounts' required for first time in Britain. *Accounting Research* first published (last issue 1958).		Communist *coup d'état* in Czechoslovakia. End of British mandate in Palestine; state of Israel proclaimed and invaded by Arab states. Berlin Blockade and Airlift.
1949			North Atlantic Treaty Organisation established.

160 MANAGEMENT ACCOUNTING

Date	Accounting	Economic Theory, Law Taxation and Management	Political Environment
			Communist victory in China. Devaluation of sterling from U.S. $4·03 to U.S. $2·80. Federal and Democratic Republics established in West and East Germany.
1950–3			Korean War.
1951	Edinburgh, Glasgow and Aberdeen Societies combine to form The Institute of Chartered Accountants of Scotland. Union Européenne des Experts Comptables, Économiques et Financiers (U.E.C.) founded. American Institute of (Certified Public) Accountants Committee on Auditing Procedure, *Codification of Statements on Auditing Procedure*.	Joel Dean, *Managerial Economics* (New York) and *Capital Budgeting* (New York).	Churchill becomes British Prime Minister for second time (until 1955). France, W. Germany, Italy, Belgium, Netherlands and Luxembourg ('the Six') sign Paris treaty, embodying the Schuman Plan to set up a single coal and steel authority.
1952	*Changing Concepts of Business Income* (Report of Study Group on Business Income of the American Institute of (Certified Public) Accountants). Australian Society of Accountants formed as result of merger of Commonwealth and Federal Institutes of Accountants.		Eisenhower elected President of U.S.A. Egyptian revolution.

Date	Accounting	Economic Theory, Law Taxation and Management	Political Environment
1953	Accounting Research Bulletin No. 43 issued by American Institute of (Certified Public) Accountants; codifies and supersedes first 42 Bulletins.		Death of Stalin; rise of Krushchev. Rising against Communist government in E. Berlin.
1954	American Institute of (Certified Public) Accountants Committee on Auditing Procedure, *Generally Accepted Auditing Standards: Their Significance and Scope*. *South African Accountant* first published. First professor of accounting at an Australian university (Sir Alexander Fitzgerald, Melbourne).		Battle of Dien Bien Phu.
1956			Suez Crisis. Hungarian Revolution.
1957	Society of Incorporated Accountants integrated with the three U.K. Chartered Institutes. American Institute of Accountants changes its name to American Institute of Certified Public Accountants; National Association of Cost Accountants changes its name to National Association of Accountants.		*Sputnik I* launched into space by U.S.S.R.

Date	Accounting	Economic Theory, Law Taxation and Management	Political Environment
1958	*Accounting Research* ceases publication.		De Gaulle elected President of France; Fifth Republic; franc devalued. European Economic Community comes into being following ratification of Treaty of Rome (1957).
1959		E. Solomon (ed.), *The Management of Corporate Capital* (New York).	European Free Trade Association established.
1960			Congo Crisis. J. F. Kennedy elected President of U.S.A.
1961	American Institute of Certified Public Accountants, *Accounting Research and Terminology Bulletins. Final Edition.* American Institute of Certified Public Accountants issues first *Accounting Research Study*.		Yuri Gagarin of U.S.S.R. becomes first space-man. South Africa becomes independent republic outside the British Commonwealth. Berlin Wall constructed.
1962	First International Conference on Accounting Education held at Urbana, Illinois. Controllers Institute of American changes its name to Financia Executives Institute. Rochdale Committee's Report on British Docks recommends use of replacement cost depreciation.	Capital gains tax introduced in Britain for first time.	Cuba Crisis.

AN ACCOUNTING CHRONOLOGY 163

Date	Accounting	Economic Theory, Law Taxation and Management	Political Environment
1963	*Journal of Accounting Research* first published.	R. M. Cyert and J. G. March, *A Behavioral Theory of the Firm*.	Britain refused entry to Common Market. Assassination of President Kennedy.
1964	*Management Services* first published.	*Journal of Management Studies* first published.	Fall of Krushchev.
1965	*Abacus*, *International Journal of Accounting* and *South African Chartered Accountant* first published.	U.K. Finance Act introduces a new corporation tax and an extended capital gains tax. Manchester and London Business Schools established.	Death of Churchill. India–Pakistan War.
1966	*Journal UEC* first published.		Dr Verwoerd, Prime Minister of South Africa, assassinated.

Index to Part One

Accounting profession: influence on capital-expenditure decisions, 57–8
Accounting rate of return, 48–50, 55–7
'Actual' cost, 21
Actuarial science, 34, 38
Alchian, A. A., 47n., 50–1
Alfred, A. M., 56
Annual cost method, 43
Arnold, H. L.: objects of cost accounting, 22
Ashley, W. J.: favours 'business economics', 17, 29n.
Avoidable cost, 16

Babbage, C., 60
Barton, A. D., 71n.
Baxter, W. T., 31
Bigg, W. W., 31
Böhm-Bawerk, A. von, 43–4
Bond tables, 38–9, 58
Bostock, C., 11–12
Boulding, K., 45–6, 53
Break-even charts, 59, 62–72
Brockie, M. D., 55n.
Brown, F. H. S., 56n.

Cannan, E.: practical usefulness of economic theory, 16, 21
Capital rationing, 50, 55
Church, A. Hamilton, 21–2
Clark, J. M., 26–8, 33
Coase, R. H., 30–1, 48, 57
Compound interest, 34–6
Control function of accounting, 11–12, 63–5
Corner, D. C., 56n.
Cost accounting: influence of financial accounting on, 21; lack of influence of economic theory on, 20–1; renaissance of, 19–20

Cost concepts for decision-making, 15–33. *See also* Avoidable cost, Differential cost, Incremental cost, Marginal cost, Opportunity cost, Variable cost
Cost of capital, 48, 52–3
Cournot, A., 17

Davenport, H. J., 18–19
Dean, J., 32, 49–50
Departmental accounting, 30–1
de Roover, R., 59
Devine, C. T., 32
Differential cost, 15, 20, 23–5, 29
Discounted cash flow: contribution of actuarial science, 34–9; contribution of engineering economy, 39–43; contribution of political economy, 43–9; developments in 1950s and 1960s, 49–57; late acceptance in practice, 57–8
Dodson, J., 37–8, 57
Double-entry book-keeping, 35, 59

Earley, J. S., 32
Ebersole, J. F., 49
Economic theory: contribution to capital budgeting, 43–55; lack of influence on cost accounting, 20–1
Edwards, R. S., 19–20n., 29–30, 38n., 56n.
Eisner, R., 55–6
Emerson, H., 22–3, 67
Engineers: break-even charts, 62–5, 67–72; capital budgeting, 39–43; influence on cost and management accounting, 11, 23–5
Equitable Life Assurance Society, 38
Evans, J. B., 56

Fells, J. M., 20, 60–1

INDEX TO PART ONE

Fermat, P. de, 37
Financial accounting: influence of, on cost and management accounting, 21, 31
Fish, J. C. F., 42–3
Fisher, I., 39, 43–7
Fisherian rate of return, 45–7, 50–1
Fixed cost, 24–6, 30, 59–72
Flexible budgeting, 67–70
Frankel, S. H., 48

Gaines, Morrell W., 11, 23–5
Garcke, E., 20, 60–1
Garner, S. P., 20n., 27n.
Goldman, O. B., 42
Gort, M., 49
Grant, E. L., 42–3
Graunt, J., 37
Green, D. I., 18–19
Grey, A. L., Jr, 55n.

Hadley, A. T., 61–2
Hagger, A. J., 54
Halley, E., 37
Harrison, G. Charter, 21, 22
Harrisons of Liverpool, 39n.
Hart, H., 56
Henderson, H., 48–9
Hess, H., 62–5, 67, 69, 72
Hirshleifer, J., 51, 54
Historical costs: irrelevance of, 17–18, 41
Horngren, C. T., 33
Hoskold, H. D., 39n.
Huygens, C., 37

Incremental cost, 30, 33
Institute of Actuaries, 38
Institute of Cost and Works Accountants, 27n., 32
Interest on capital, 27–8
Interest rates: influence of on investment decisions, 48–9
Interest tables, 35–6
Internal rate of return, 38–9, 45–55, 58

Istvan, D. F., 55–6

Jaedicke, R. K., 33
Jevons, W. S., 17–18
Johnston, J., 71n.
Joint costs, 28
Judd, H. G., 23, 25–6

Karmel, P. H., 54n.
Keynes, J. M., 45–7, 50
Knoeppel, C. E., 67–70, 72

Lardner, D., 60
Lawson, G. H., 56
Lehfeldt, R. A., 48
Leonardo of Pisa, 34–5
Life assurance, 37–8
Linear programming and break-even analysis, 72
Loder, R.: farm accounts 1610–20, 15–16
Lorie, J. H., 52–3, 55
Lutz, F. and V., 50

Machlup, F., 71
Mann, Sir John, 65–6, 69, 72
Marginal cost, 17, 19, 20
Marginal efficiency of capital, *see* Internal rate of return
Marginal rate of return over cost, 45, 47
Marshall, A., 43–4, 61
Mathematical-programming approach to capital budgeting, 55
May, G. O., 21n.
Medici, Francesco di Guiliano di Raffaello de', & Co., 59
Merrett, A. J., 56
Minor, A. J., 70–1
Moore, C. L., 33
Mortality statistics, 37
Multiple rates of return, 46–7, 50, 52–5
Murdoch, W., 16
Mutually exclusive investments, 50–51

INDEX TO PART ONE

National Association of (Cost) Accountants, 27n., 32
National Economic Development Council, 57
Neild, R. D., 56
Neo-classical economics, 16–19
Net present value, 36, 40–5, 47–8, 51–4, 57
Neuner, J. J. W., 28–9

Opportunity cost, 16, 18, 29, 32
Overhead allocation, 21–2, 25, 30

Pacioli, L., 35, 57
Pascal, B., 37
Past costs: irrelevance of, 17–18, 41
Payback period, 49, 55–7
Pegolotti, F. B., 35
Pennell, W. O., 40
Pitchford, J. D., 54
Political economy, *see* Economic theory
Pollard, S., 16n., 20n.
Price, J. M., 38
Pricing policy, 25, 30, 65
Probability, mathematical theory of, 37
Production centres, 21–2
Profitability yield, 50
Profitgraph, *see* Break-even chart
Profit-volume charts, 71
Prussman, D. F., 56

Railway economics, 39–40, 60
Rate of interest: influence on investment decisions, 48–9
Rate of return, *see* Accounting rate of return; Internal rate of return
Rate of return on sacrifice, 45
Rate of return over cost, 45–7, 50–1
Rautenstrauch, W., 67, 69–72
Renshaw, E., 53–4

Samuelson, P. A., 45, 53

Savage, L. J., 52–3, 55
Scott, W. P., 56
Senior, N., 60
Shillinglaw, G., 33
Single investments, 46, 52–4
Solomon, E., 53–4
Solomons, D., 20, 32
Soper, C. S., 54n.
South African Mining Industry Commission, 48
Standard costing, 12, 22–3, 67
Stevin, S., 35–6, 57–8
Stewardship function of accounting, 11–12
Sykes, A., 56

Todhunter, R., 39
Torrens, R., 60
Trenchant, J., 35

Van Deventer, J. H., 41
Variable cost, 24–6, 30, 59–72
Vatter, W. J., 29, 32
'Vestance', 42

Weaver, J. B., 55n.
Weingartner, H. M., 55
Wellington, A. M., 23, 39–40
Whitmore, J., 22
Wicksell, K., 43
Wicksteed, P. H., 19
Wieser, F. von, 18
Wiles, P. J. D., 71
Williams, A., 56n.
Williams, B. R., 56
Williams, J. B., 47–8
Williams, J. H., 67, 70, 72
Witt, J. de, 37
Witt, R., 36
Wright, J. F., 54n.

Yamey, B. S., 15

ST. MARY'S COLLEGE OF MARYLAND
   ST. MARY'S CITY, MARYLAND

40195